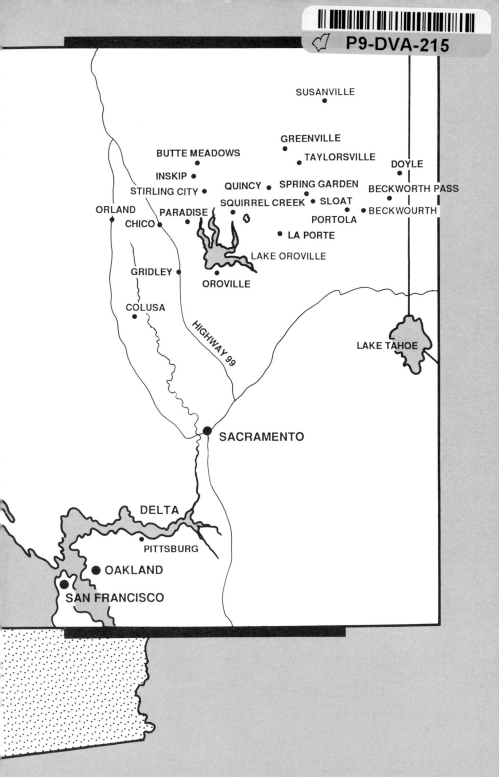

SUSANVILLE

GREENVILLE

BUTTE MEADOWS

TAYLORSVILLE

DOYLE

INSKIP

QUINCY   SPRING GARDEN

BECKWORTH PASS

STIRLING CITY

SQUIRREL CREEK   SLOAT

BECKWOURTH

ORLAND

PARADISE

CHICO

PORTOLA

LA PORTE

LAKE OROVILLE

GRIDLEY

OROVILLE

COLUSA

HIGHWAY 99

LAKE TAHOE

SACRAMENTO

DELTA

PITTSBURG

OAKLAND

SAN FRANCISCO

SABERTOOTH

To Jerry Farmer, with best wishes. Hope you enjoy SABERTOOTH.

Jerry Hodges

To my wife, Cathy, for her love and encouragement, and for her many hours of help on this project.

Special thanks to Joe Graziano, whose friendship has made a great difference in my life.

SABERTOOTH

THE RIP-ROARING ADVENTURES OF A LEGENDARY GAME WARDEN

TERRY HODGES

T&C BOOKS
OROVILLE, CALIFORNIA

SABERTOOTH
The Rip-Roaring Adventures of a Legendary Game Warden
by Terry Hodges

Copy © 1988 by Terry Hodges

ISBN 0-9634092-0-4
Printed in the United States of America

Published by T&C Books
P.O. Box 1126
Oroville, CA 95965
(916) 533-0698

Personalized copies, signed by author, are available.
Direct inquiries and/or orders to the above address.

Cover illustration by Bill Border.

Contents

Preface

I never set out to write a book. It just sort of happened by accident. Actually it happened because of my love for my work and my appreciation for good game wardens . . . and because I found myself with a story that needed telling, and no one else to tell it.

I was hired as a California Fish and Game Warden in the fall of 1972. Since then I've been fascinated by tales of certain of my predecessors, the hard-nosed, old-time wardens who prowled California in years past. Men like Lee Sinkey, who had an arm shot off in a confrontation with poachers, but went on to make the arrest. Or Gene Durney, who swam a hundred yards one dark night, to battle his way aboard a net boat and capture a dangerous pair of Delta outlaws. These wardens were men who knew *exactly* their purpose in life, men who genuinely loved the wildlife they were sworn to protect, men who took it personally when wildlife was abused. These were men I admired.

Among these best of the old timers—the ones whose names are most often heard whenever wardens speak with reverence of the truly great ones of their profession—was Gene Mercer, the one they called Old Sabertooth.

I was a rookie warden when I first heard of Old Sabertooth, and it was a story I will never forget. It was the story of a man who hadn't just *worked* as a warden, but who had *lived* his profession every minute of every day for over thirty years—a man who found it impossible to compromise his standards even in the face of direct orders from above.

The Fish and Game Division was changing. The job of game warden was changing, and Mercer was finding it difficult to adapt. The state was placing restrictions on the hours he could work, insisting that he take two full days off each week. He was dismayed and outraged. Warden work was his life, protecting wildlife his obsession, and he saw no way he could turn his back on his responsibilities for even *one* day a week, let alone two. And so, to the chagrin of his supervisors in Sacramento, he ignored the new policy and continued to work seven days a week. There followed a running battle between Mercer and Willard Greenwald, the Patrol Inspector in the Sacramento office at the time. Greenwald would order Mercer to take his days off, and Mercer would stubbornly ignore him and work anyway. Finally, Greenwald got fed up with the situation and made the two-hour drive to Chico to settle the matter face to face with the old warden. But when Greenwald arrived in Chico, Mercer refused to see him . . . because it was his day off.

This was a man I had to meet.

In 1976, I transferred to Mercer's old patrol district to become the Oroville warden. I'll never forget the first time I saw him—or rather the first time he saw *me*, the new man who had come to take over a piece of his beloved county. He looked me over with the most intense gaze I've ever experienced, scrutinizing me as though I had come courting his daughter. It was a cool reception at best, but I knew that Gene Mercer didn't squander his friendship on just anybody. I would have to earn it.

He was in his late seventies then, but in my mind

he never seemed over sixty. He was strong and agile for his age—and if you put him in a green patrol car, the years seemed to melt off him like magic. I could never think of him as retired—as anything but a warden—for in fact he remains to this day a game warden through and through.

I got a surprise when he rode with me on the opening day of my first deer season in the mountains above Oroville. I expected him to sit passively in my truck and watch me work, but that's not what happened. He was out on every stop, talking to hunters, checking licenses and deer tags, and looking in vehicles for illegal game or loaded rifles. Although he was in civilian clothes and wore no badge, he conveyed such an air of authority, such complete confidence, that no one ever questioned his actions—least of all me.

Patrolling with Mercer was a real education. Not only did he know every inch of my patrol district, but he had an uncanny understanding of the wildlife—an understanding born of love. And then there were the stories—fascinating tales of past adventures, of the way things used to be, stories that came in an unending flow as though he had waited twenty years for someone to listen. I felt I was being allowed a rare glimpse into the past, at some precious bit of history that was on the brink of being lost forever.

It was out of a sense of responsibility that I started taking notes—notes I was certain would be of value to some future author. But I got carried away in my note taking, and now, two years later, I find *myself* the author. The result of my efforts is a modest work at best, but I feel good about it, for it was a job that needed doing.

In the following collection of stories, I speak of Mercer at his best, *doing* what he liked best. It's not my intention to portray him as some faultless hero, for like all of us, he had his shortcomings. Nor do I intend to detract in any way from the excellent work of other good wardens. But to portray Gene Mercer as anything less than one of the very best wardens that ever lived would be to do him a grave disservice.

Dollar-a-Year Man

"You say they're killin' bighorns?" asked Captain Ed Ober of the California Division of Fish and Game.

"That's right," replied the slender young man in ranch-hand's garb. "They've been up there for over a week."

Captain Ober scrutinized the bearer of this information, and the young man returned his gaze with steady, penetrating brown eyes.

"Can you take us to their camp?" asked Ober.

"Yes," the young man answered. "I can get you there."

Ober arranged to meet the young man the following morning at the Lone Tree Ranch where he worked, several miles north of Bishop. Then, as Ober turned to go, he hesitated and faced the young man again. "What did you say your name was?" he asked.

"Eugene Mercer," replied the young man. "But people call me Gene."

*　　　　*　　　　*

It was the summer of 1927, and Gene Mercer, at age twenty-six, was not a happy man. It seemed that his life up to that point had been something of a failure.

He had left home at seventeen and tried several jobs, including four years working as a locomotive fireman for Southern Pacific Railroad. Then things turned sour. When he tried his hand at farming, purchasing a small farm in Madera County, a bad drought and other bad luck turned the venture into a disaster. Deeply in debt, he was forced to sell out at a loss and move back to the Lone Tree Ranch, in Mono County, where he had been born and raised. Now he was back where he had started, facing the dismal prospect of supporting a wife and paying off his debts on ranch-hand's wages.

No, he wasn't happy, but at least his job on the Lone Tree Ranch was pleasant outdoor work, and the setting was magnificent. The old ranch, homesteaded years earlier by his grandfather, was nestled against the game-rich western slopes of the rugged White Mountains, and the cattle shared the juniper flats with mule deer, wild horses, and antelope. High above, beyond the treeline of stunted piñons, the ragged granite ridges were home to the bighorn sheep, and Mercer thrilled to an occasional glimpse of the elusive creatures.

It was the bighorns that brought the poachers, often wealthy trophy hunters from Los Angeles. Greedy, wasteful men, they came in expensive cars and set up camp in a high, remote meadow. They arrived unnoticed, and for days the ranchers in the valley below puzzled over the occasional faint reports of their rifles.

The mystery was cleared up when the man known locally as French Pete arrived at the ranch, thoroughly outraged. Somewhat of a hermit, French Pete lived alone in a small cabin a few miles above the ranch, and earlier that morning he had yielded to curiosity and crept up on the poacher's camp. Staying out of sight, he had watched one of the men fleshing out a bighorn cape. He was greatly upset, for he knew the bighorns were protected, and he had grown fond of having them around. After sneaking away, he felt the urge to tell somebody, so he hiked on down to the ranch. The ranch people—especially Mercer—shared French Pete's fondness for bighorns, and upon hearing the news, Mercer drove the twenty-eight miles into Bishop and contacted Captain Ober.

True to his word, Captain Ober and two other wardens—Webb Talbot from Bishop and another man by the name of Prescott—pulled into the ranch at six o'clock the following morning. Mercer was waiting and immediately set out to lead them to the poacher's camp. When they had driven to within a mile of the place, they parked the car and continued on foot.

The morning sun was just topping the eastern rim as they sighted the camp at the far side of the meadow, and it was obvious that they had arrived none too soon. The poachers—four of them—were breaking camp, and in another half hour they would have been gone.

Mercer waited in a small grove of aspens as Ober whispered commands to Talbot and Prescott, who nodded and hurried away, keeping well out of sight. Soon they were positioned around the camp, and at Ober's signal they made their move. The surprise of the poachers was complete, and as the three armed officers walked in on them, they made no move to resist. Mercer studied the wardens as they went about their work, calm and businesslike, and he envied them, thinking it must be a great adventure to be a game warden.

Later that day, Mercer had the chance to examine the evidence the wardens had seized. There were four expensive rifles and the heads and capes of three bighorn rams. He studied the ram heads with awe, fascinated by their massive, curled horns. One magnificent specimen, old and battle-scarred, had horns that had grown well beyond a full curl. Mercer was sickened at the thought of the old warrior falling victim to poachers.

While Mercer studied the ram heads, Captain Ober was studying him. Ober considered himself a good judge of men, and he had positive feelings about Mercer.

"Gene, have you ever considered being a volunteer

game warden?" he asked.

Mercer looked up in surprise. Until that moment, he hadn't been aware that there even *was* such a thing as a volunteer game warden, but the idea was immediately appealing to him. Ober went on to explain that the purpose of volunteer wardens was to assist the regular wardens in their work, and he emphasized the point that volunteer wardens received absolutely no pay for their time. Mercer's only question was "How do I get to be one?"

A few days later in Bishop, Mercer was sworn in by Captain Ober, who issued him his badge, a bronze shield stamped "Division of Fish and Game, Volunteer Warden." Mercer was delighted. He had become what was known in those days as a dollar-a-year man ... and he was about to get a taste of what was to become his life's work.

The Chance
of a Lifetime

Gene Mercer stood in the little post office, stunned, staring down at the telegram he held with trembling hands. It was such a small thing, a few printed words on a scrap of paper, yet he knew that his life would be forever changed by it. He read through it again, hardly daring to believe the words, then he turned and walked out into the sunlight. He gazed up at the snowcapped Sierras rising majestically to the west, and breathing deeply, he drank in the sweet smells of spring. The world had never seemed quite so beautiful.

It was April of 1928. Seven months had passed since he had helped the wardens capture the bighorn poachers and had become a volunteer warden. His association with the wardens had made his life a little brighter, but there had been precious little time to spend with them.

He had helped them on the opening weekend of trout season when he, Warden Webb Talbot, and another warden spent two days at Adobe Meadows, near the Nevada border, patrolling the trout streams and checking fishermen. There had been violations—mainly Nevada citizens fishing without licenses or in possession of overlimits of trout—and the wardens had made about a dozen arrests. While it was no big thing to the regular wardens, Mercer had enjoyed the experience immensely.

But, aside from that weekend and a few other outings with the wardens, Mercer had been basically unhappy and dissatisfied with his life. He was still stuck on the ranch, in debt, and his meager salary of sixty dollars a month guaranteed that he would remain that way for a long time. Then came the telegram.

Edna Mercer was startled when, suddenly, the door to their cabin burst open and her husband came rushing in, grinning widely, a telegram in his hand.

"Take a look at this," he said excitedly, thrusting the paper into her hands. It was from Assistant Chief of Patrol Milt Clark of the California Division of Fish and Game. It read:

> IF YOU ARE INTERESTED IN BECOMING A FULL TIME FISH AND GAME WARDEN, REPORT TO CAPTAIN JOSEPH SANDERS AT PORTOLA BY THE FIRST OF MAY. THE JOB PAYS $125 PER MONTH.

When Edna reached the part about the salary, her eyes lit up, and soon she was in nearly as good a mood as her husband. Before the day was over, they had begun to pack.

Mercer had never considered becoming a game warden. The thought had simply never occurred to him. But when the telegram arrived, the realization that he actually had a chance of becoming a warden had a tremendous impact on him. He became obsessed with the idea and could think of little else.

Later, when his pulse had returned to something approaching normal, he was puzzled over the whole thing. Why had he received such a telegram? He had never applied to become a warden, nor had he ever expressed any such interest to the wardens he knew ... and he had never heard of Assistant Chief of Patrol Milt Clark. It wasn't until more than a year later that he learned of a chance meeting in San Francisco between his mother and her old schoolmate Milt Clark.

*   *   *

The old Model T Ford growled along, engine straining, as it clawed its way up the steep, rutted track known as the Sherwin Grade. A few miles north of Bishop, this tortuous piece of roadway that zigzagged up and over a high mountain ridge had proven fatal to many an automotive engine over the years. Today it appeared that it was about to claim another victim.

At the wheel of the old Ford, Gene Mercer was filled with dread as again he heard the unwelcome rattle of an ailing rod bearing in the vehicle's overstressed engine. The day before, at practically the same spot, he and Edna had been forced to turn around and limp back to Bishop where a mechanic had replaced a bad bearing. In view of their financial situation, it had been a grim piece of luck. Now it looked as if they were in trouble again.

Mercer pulled over and stopped, thoroughly frustrated. Edna was on the verge of tears. Their situation was serious now, for they were nearly out of cash, and it didn't look as though the crippled old Ford would get them to Portola by the May 1 deadline. Mercer was deeply concerned that he wouldn't make it on time and Captain Sanders would fill the warden position with someone else.

But right about then, their luck took a turn for the better. In the distance, a Standard Oil tank truck appeared, lumbering up the mountain. The driver had problems of his own as the heavy vehicle bucked and reeled up the rugged track, and when he passed the stranded Mercers, he spared them hardly a glance. He was so intent on his driving that he failed to notice when a sealed five-gallon pail bounced out of the rear of his vehicle and came to rest, undamaged, in a chuckhole. Mercer called out and tried to attract his attention, but the truck never slowed, growling on and out of sight over the ridge.

Mercer walked over to examine the pail and found it to contain motor oil. Standing there looking down at it, he suddenly had an idea. Perhaps, if he totally filled the crankcase of the Model T with oil, he could make the engine hold together a while longer. But would it run? Deciding that he had little to lose, he added a few more quarts of oil and tried the engine. To his surprise, it started immediately and sounded a little better than before.

Soon he and Edna were on their way again, creeping along in low gear, nursing the tired old engine up the grade. Their luck held, and they made it to the top. From there on it was easy going, and nightfall found them in Carson City, Nevada. The following morning they got an early start and by noon they were well past Reno and back in California again, picking their way over Beckworth Pass. An hour later, they pulled into Portola.

That evening they met Captain Joseph Sanders, and Mercer liked him immediately. Upon examining the telegram, Sanders looked at Mercer with a smile.

"You're a lucky man," he said. "Do you have any idea how tough it is to get one of these jobs?"

"I guess I don't," Mercer replied.

"Well, it's real tough," Sanders continued. "But there are some things you should know before you make a commitment. Being a game warden is more than just a job—it's a way of life. You'll live with it twenty-four hours a day, seven days a week. And you'll get called out day and night. It's not easy on a family man, for you'll often be away from home for long periods of time. You'll have to get used to being cold and wet and tired, because you'll be that way a lot. And it's not the safest profession in the world, either. There are some bad folks out there that you'll have to face ... people with guns. They'll hate you for carrying a warden's badge, and they'll kill you if you give 'em half a chance."

Sanders was carefully watching Mercer's eyes for any

sign of doubt or weakness. There was none.

"But it's also the best job in the world," he continued, smiling again. "Do you think you can handle it?"

"I can handle it," Mercer replied without hesitation.

"Then I guess you've got yourself a job," said Sanders, and Mercer's spirits soared.

*   *   *

Sensing, and fully understanding, Mercer's intense curiosity to know more about his new job, Sanders spent more than two hours with him that night, poring over maps of the patrol district for which Mercer would be responsible and discussing warden work in general. Sanders then gave him a Fish and Game code book and a citation book and some instructions on their use. By the time the two men parted company that night, Mercer's head was swimming with new information.

The following day, April 27, 1928, Mercer stood before Judge Long in Portola, his right hand raised, and he was sworn in. At the end of the ceremony, Captain Sanders presented him with his badge, a shiny, five-pointed star of nickel silver, and Mercer was thrilled. He would treasure the badge, for it was the symbol of his new life—an exciting new life with a purpose.

Later that afternoon, while exploring some of the country near town, Mercer spotted some deer browsing near the river. It dawned on him then that those deer, and all the other wildlife for miles around, had become his own special responsibility. He was filled with pride at the thought, and for the first time in his twenty-seven years, he knew, with absolute certainty, that he was *exactly* where he wanted to be.

The Price of Greed

Randle Moak's cane fly rod hissed through the air, sending the greased line shooting out across the clear waters of Red Clover Creek. The tapered leader turned nicely and the gaily-colored Royal Coachman alighted gently at the head of a deep riffle. The fly danced on the surface as it was swept along, then suddenly the water beneath it erupted in a violent swirl and it was gone. Moak lifted the rod tip and set the hook, and a few minutes later slid another foot-long, honey-colored brown trout into his already bulging creel. He was aware that he had already exceeded the twenty-five-fish trout limit, but conditions on the stream were perfect, and he was having too much fun to quit. Besides, he knew that a careful man who took the right precautions had little reason to worry about the law.

*   *   *

The sunlight was bright on the slopes of Mount Ingalls as Warden Gene Mercer drove along, enjoying what was turning out to be a beautiful spring morning. The road he traveled meandered down a timbered ridge as it made its slow descent to the Genesee Valley below. Rounding a bend, he encountered a car parked at the edge of the pines.

"Must belong to a fisherman," he thought, as he pulled to a stop. Walking up to the vehicle, he took a look inside and spotted an empty fly rod case on the floor near the back seat. Craning his neck, he examined the registration card in its little holder on the steering column.

"Randle T. Moak," he muttered, as he read from the card. "Moak . . . Moak . . . ," he repeated as he pondered the name. It had a familiar ring to it. Then it dawned on him—Captain Sanders had told him to keep a close eye on anybody by that name, for the Moaks were well-known poachers in Plumas County.

Mercer turned his car around and drove a few hundred yards back the way he had come. There was no place to hide the vehicle, but at least the fisherman wouldn't be able to see it unless he went looking for it—which was a possibility. But Mercer, in his short career, was learning that a warden could rarely cover *all* the possibilities.

Going back on foot, he passed Moak's car and continued down the ridge another hundred yards or so. Picking a spot just off the road, he settled down to wait. From there, he could still see Moak's car, and he could also see portions of the trail, which zigzagged down into the canyon to Red Clover Creek.

Leaning back against a granite boulder, he gazed up at the rugged slopes of Mount Ingalls, its craggy granite ridges and pine-choked canyons thrusting upward to pierce a sky of intense blue. Mercer regarded it all with deep appreciation and a wave of euphoria swept over him. It was a feeling he had experienced often during the past year, his first as a warden, and he couldn't imagine being any happier.

He had been extremely lucky in his first duty assignment. The Portola position was a prime patrol district, encompassing parts of Plumas, Lassen, and Sierra counties—some of the most beautiful country in northern California. Much of it was mountainous and forested, but there were also vast expanses of sage-scattered high desert, as well as hundreds of miles of prime trout streams and thousands of square miles of both summer and winter mule deer ranges. It was a wonderful setting for a warden to begin his career.

Like all new wardens, Mercer started work with virtually no training. The captain simply provided him with some basic tools, a little advice, and sent him on his way. And like all new wardens, he experienced an odd mixture of feelings and emotions, ranging from extreme exhilaration to severe frustration and everything in between. He learned largely through trial and error, like a young fox learning to hunt, but he learned quickly, assembling the bits and pieces of knowledge and experience that would eventually make him a highly respected warden.

As the months passed and he got the feel of his new job, he came to realize that he was doing what he truly wanted to do. He found that he not only loved every aspect of warden work, but that he indeed had a special talent for it—a fact that quickly became apparent to game-law violators, who found the new warden to be not only cunning and resourceful, but totally committed to his work.

And so it was that Mercer, on this sunny morning on the ridge above Red Clover Creek, was no longer a green rookie. While not a veteran by any means, he was competent, and what he lacked in knowledge and experience, he more than made up for with enthusiasm and boundless energy. But he was patient as well, which served him well in this work.

It turned out to be a four-hour wait before he spotted the fisherman, rod in hand, hiking up the trail out of the canyon. Mercer watched as the man made his way up the steep trail. Near the top of the ridge, the trees grew thicker, and Mercer could catch only an occasional glimpse of him. But he noticed that the man stopped for a couple of minutes when still some distance from his car. He apparently knelt down and was out of sight during this time, and Mercer took pains to pick out landmarks that would later guide him to the spot.

When Moak reached his car, he leaned his rod against a tree and slipped off his creel. Then something caught his attention, and he walked over and studied the surface of the road a few yards from his car.

"Damn," thought Mercer. "He sees where I turned around."

Sure enough, Moak suddenly looked up and glanced nervously around, looking first up the road toward where Mercer's car was parked, then scanning the forest near his own car. Apparently not satisfied, he loaded his gear into his car and drove up the road, following the suspicious vehicle tracks. He soon found Mercer's car and, somewhat shaken, turned around and headed back down the mountain. Mercer, in the meantime, had trotted up to the spot where Moak had been parked, and he met the man coming back down the road. Standing in the road and displaying his badge, Mercer forced Moak to stop.

"State game warden," announced Mercer, approaching the driver's window. "How was the fishing this morning?"

"Pretty good," Moak answered, forcing a smile. "It took me a while, but I got my limit."

"Well, I'd like to see your fish, if you don't mind, and I'd also like to have a look at your fishing license," said Mercer.

Moak turned off the engine and stepped out, fumbling for his wallet and his fishing license. Mercer noticed that the man's hands were trembling slightly. After Mercer examined the license, Moak pulled his wicker creel from the back seat and presented it to the warden. Mercer removed the trout, one or two at a time, from their bed of grass and fern fronds and laid them out on a large rock. It was a beautiful mixed catch of browns and rainbows, twenty-five of them, all longer than eleven inches. Mercer delighted in the sweet, fresh-trout smell.

"Do you have any other fish?" asked Mercer.

"No," answered Moak, a little too quickly. "That's all I've got."

Carefully watching Moak's eyes, Mercer said, "Well, I noticed that you stopped a ways back when you were coming up the trail. What were you doing?"

Averting his eyes and again forcing a smile, Moak answered, "I had to water a pine tree, that's all. Why? What's the matter?"

"Oh, no problem," said Mercer, "Just doin' my job. Would you mind taking a little walk down there with me?"

Moak hesitated a second or two. "Sure ... I'll go with you," he said, knowing full well that he had little choice.

Mercer had no trouble locating the landmarks he was looking for, but when he arrived at the spot where Moak had stopped, he found nothing. Moving off the trail, he searched back under the trees. Still nothing. He scrutinized the ground for signs of the spot where Moak had left the trail, but the hard, rock-strewn surface offered no clues. Then, bewildered, he stood back a moment to think. Moak stood quietly nearby, and Mercer suddenly became aware of the silence. It was a still, quiet afternoon—totally silent except for the soft buzzing of insects.

"Insects!" thought Mercer, quickly swiveling his head to focus on the sound. Near the base of a pine tree there were several large, metallic-black blowflies circling busily over the carpet of pine needles. As Mercer approached the spot, he could see that the pine needles had been disturbed. Reaching down, he swept the needles aside, and there lay a bundle of trout, fifteen of them, wrapped in a large bandanna. Moak stood staring at the ground, muttering curses to himself as Mercer picked up the fish.

"Let's go," said Mercer, directing Moak back up the trail.

Randle Moak had little to say as he received his citation for the overlimit of trout. He had simply been outsmarted, and he would take his lumps without complaint. Later, as he drove home, without a single trout to show for his day's efforts, he had to admit to himself that he had gained a new respect for game wardens.

Mixed Emotions

One summer day, around 1930, Mercer set out in his old Model T to investigate a tip that deer were being illegally killed and sold in the mountain country west of Doyle. Turning north at Chilcoot, from what is now Highway 70, he started up the winding and rutted dirt road that would take him to the Meadowview Ranger Station. There was a good chance the rangers there might have heard something about the poaching.

It would have been difficult to spot Mercer as a game warden as he traveled along on that summer morning, for it was at least seven years prior to the time when the Fish and Game Division would equip its wardens with either state patrol cars or uniforms. Mercer patrolled in his own car, and the state reimbursed him at six cents a mile on good roads and eight cents a mile when the roads were bad ... which was most of the time. He wore comfortable clothing: denim pants, flannel shirt, hat, vest (which concealed his badge), and lace-up boots. He looked more like a lumberman or rancher than a game warden.

Because the old road took him through miles of mountainous summer cattle range, he was forced to stop often to open and close gates. It was during one of these brief stops that he heard a car coming his way from the north. Since it would be a good idea to talk to the driver and get a look inside the car, Mercer stayed at the gate where the approaching vehicle would have to stop.

Reaching into his car, he grabbed the borrowed 32/20 revolver off the front seat and thrust it into his waistband beneath his vest. This was odd behavior for him, for he hated packing a gun (sidearms were optional for wardens at that time). Later, he would be unable to explain why, on this occasion, he chose to carry the weapon.

Just then, the approaching car wheeled into view, and Mercer was quick to notice its Nevada plates. It was a shiny new Chandler, one of the open touring cars of the day. A well dressed, middle-aged man was at the wheel, and a somewhat younger but equally well dressed woman shared the front seat with him. Two young girls about ten and twelve years old occupied the back seat.

As the vehicle pulled to a stop facing him, Mercer noticed that the driver had an unpleasant look on his face, obviously not pleased with the delay. Mercer smiled and gave a little wave as he started walking toward the vehicle, but the driver held up his hand in warning and told Mercer in a stern voice to stay away from the car. When Mercer continued his approach, the driver—suddenly quite nervous—raised his voice and said, "I'm warning you, mister, stay away from this car."

But Mercer continued on, playing dumb and asking questions. "I just need some help ... can you tell me where this road comes out?" asked Mercer, but the other man, now highly agitated, shouted at Mercer to stay away.

Mercer covered the last few feet to the driver's door in time to see the man reach quickly under the front seat and bring out a pistol. Mercer was surprised, but managed to beat the man to the draw, and as the man turned in his seat to bring the gun to bear, Mercer clubbed him a sharp blow to the head with the old

32/20 revolver. The woman screamed, the young girls shrieked, and the man slumped forward, unconscious and bleeding.

"You've killed him," cried the woman, and Mercer, for one uncomfortable moment, had the terrible feeling that she was right—that he'd provoked the man and killed him, in front of his family, for no good reason.

A gash on the man's head bled profusely, and he was soon a gory sight, with blood smeared and running down his face and dripping onto his clothes. The woman, upon discovering herself blood-spattered as well, screamed all the louder, and the girls increased the volume of their wailing. Mercer, now nearly deafened, pulled out his handkerchief and applied it to the man's wound. The man, to Mercer's vast relief, was now showing signs of life.

"I'm a state game warden, ma'am," said Mercer, hoping to calm the woman. "This man's gonna be all right."

It was about this time that Mercer spotted something under a tarp on the floor in the back seat—something the girls had been resting their feet on. Mercer turned back one corner of the tarp, revealing the carcass of a doe. Wasting no time, he grabbed the deer, hauled it out of the Chandler, and piled it into his own car. He then returned to the Chandler and located the man's revolver, which had dropped to the floorboards. He grabbed the weapon and tossed it onto the front seat of the Model T.

The man had by then regained consciousness and was gingerly fingering the wound on his head. Mercer informed him that he was under arrest and escorted him over to the Model T, intending to drive the man to jail and allow the woman to drive the girls home in the Chandler. But the woman provided him with a dilemma by informing him that she didn't know how to drive.

Faced with the problem of what to do about the woman and girls, Mercer came up with a plan: He would take the woman with him in the Model T—as sort of a hostage—and allow the man to follow him back to town in the Chandler.

It seemed like a reasonable idea, and for a while it worked out fine, for the woman attended to the opening and closing of the many gates. But at the last gate, where the countryside had flattened out considerably near the highway, Mercer's plan went awry. The woman got out, opened the gate, and stood there as Mercer drove through. But when the man drove the Chandler through, the woman jumped onto the running board and the man gunned the engine. The Chandler shot forward, swerved out onto the shoulder and raced past Mercer's car. Mercer furiously gave chase, but it was soon evident that the old Model T was no match for the new Chandler. Mercer could see the young girls looking back, eyes wide with excitement, as the Chandler steadily pulled away. The warden's last view of the vehicle was of it careening around a bend, the woman still out on the running board, hanging on for dear life.

Mercer was left in the dust, terribly frustrated, and highly disgusted with himself. He had misjudged the people, allowed them too much opportunity, and now he was paying the price. He swore to himself to never make such a mistake again.

When his anger had subsided somewhat, Mercer thought back through the incident and concluded that he hadn't done all that badly after all. He had the deer, which the man had probably purchased from the real poachers; the man would undoubtedly require several stitches to close the gash above his left ear; and he had the man's gun.

At the thought of the gun, Mercer glanced down at the shiny revolver lying on the seat beside him. It was a Smith & Wesson .38 caliber—a thing of beauty. He picked it up, marveling at the beautifully engraved nickel finish and the shiny two-and-a-half-dollar gold pieces inlaid in each of its pearl grips. It was a fascinating weapon, and as he was enjoying its satisfying heft in his hand, it suddenly dawned on him that he had become its new owner. Up to that time, he had been unable to afford the purchase of a sidearm, but now, unless the violator came back to claim the weapon—a highly unlikely possibility—he had finally acquired his own pistol. This pleasant thought left him with mixed emotions and at least temporarily took the edge off his anger.

*　　　　*　　　　*

As is often the case, Mercer learned the identity of the escaped violator a couple of months later. The man had been a doctor in Reno, and the woman, the girls, and the pearl-handled gun had been 'borrowed' from another man. After his brush with Mercer, the badly shaken doctor sold his practice and moved back to Ohio.

A Matter of Politics

Charles Lawrence Bending wasn't pleased that fall morning in 1929. It seemed that his outing in the sage country near Susanville had taken a sudden turn for the worse. Immaculately attired in his tweed gunning apparel, complete with cap and necktie, he cradled his gold-inlaid Parker double in the crook of his arm and frowned at the game warden who was counting the quail in his bulging game bag. Nearby, a matched pair of English pointers, noses to the ground, busily worked through a patch of cover that a few minutes earlier had contained a large covey of the plump little birds that seemed so plentiful. It wasn't just the interruption of his hunt that outraged Mr. Bending, a wealthy Nevada attorney. It was the suggestion of the warden that he was possibly in violation of the game laws—laws obviously intended for lesser men.

"Sir, I'm afraid you're well over your legal limit of mountain quail," said Warden Gene Mercer, looking up from his task. "May I see your hunting license, please?"

Bending grumbled to himself as he produced a resident California hunting license from his expensive leather billfold. Mercer examined the license with suspicion, recalling the Nevada plates on the new sedan parked nearby.

"Now I'll need to see your driver's license, if you don't mind," said Mercer.

Bending dug into his billfold again and reluctantly produced his Nevada driver's license.

"Is this your correct address?" Mercer asked. Bending nodded to the affirmative.

"Then you're hunting without a valid hunting license," said Mercer. "You need a nonresident license to hunt in California." Mercer had no doubts that Bending had simply attempted to get by without buying the more expensive nonresident license.

"What difference does it make?" Bending asked. "I paid for a license, what does it matter where I live?"

"It matters," stated Mercer flatly, reaching for his citation book.

"You know, I'm a good friend of your governor," said Bending, as Mercer started writing. "In fact, we grew up together."

"Should that matter?" asked Mercer, as he continued writing.

"I'm sure your governor would think I deserved a warning on this," said Bending, but Mercer was unmoved.

"I'm going to have to seize the quail and your shotgun into evidence," said Mercer. He was prepared for *any* reaction, for he suspected the man would sooner part with one of his kids than his 20-gauge Parker.

"No," said Bending, taking a step back. "You can have the quail, but you're not taking my gun."

"Oh yes," said Mercer with certainty, fixing Bending with a hard gaze. "The shotgun's going with me ... the only question is whether or not *you're* goin' with it."

The look in Mercer's eyes was enough to tell Bending that the warden would not be intimidated, so the hunter reluctantly relinquished the shotgun and signed the citation. But as he was leaving, he turned back to Mercer and said, "You'll be hearing about this."

Mercer had the disquieting feeling that the man's

words were no idle threat, for at that time, politics—the unwritten code that demanded special treatment, if not immunity from the law, for high-ranking officials, their families, and their friends—was an unpleasant fact of life. Mercer knew full well that an officer who failed to honor this corrupt system could easily find himself out of work. It wasn't until 1932 that civil service laws were enacted to protect law enforcement officers from this type of thing.

Sure enough, less than a week later, Mercer received a letter from the chief of patrol directing him to dismiss the case against Charles Bending, and return the man's quail and shotgun to him at his Reno address. Mercer was outraged and was quite vocal about it, but he didn't blame the chief. He sensed that the chief was every bit as upset over the matter as *he* was.

Now Mercer was in a quandary: Not only was it morally unacceptable to let Bending off, it would violate federal law if the quail—illegally taken game birds—were transported across the state line. He spent days pondering the problem, agonizing over the decision that could well cost him the job he had grown to love so much.

Finally, acting on the advice of some veteran forest rangers, Mercer discussed the matter with the Susanville judge. The judge, upon hearing about the situation, immediately announced that he would refuse to dismiss the case against Bending. This took most of the heat off Mercer, and the warden breathed a sigh of relief. But the fact remained that he had dragged his feet in taking care of the matter, and his job was still in jeopardy.

Despite his plea to the governor, Charles Bending ended up before the Susanville judge after all. Although his shotgun was returned to him, he paid a substantial fine.

Justice had been served, but Mercer was worried for weeks, expecting each day to find his termination letter in the mail. The letter never came. Instead, a year later, at a training meeting in San Francisco, the chief of patrol stood up before a room jammed with wardens and commended Mercer for having the grit to stand up for what he believed in.

Winter Patrol

It was a blustery winter morning in the mountain community of Quincy. Warden Gene Mercer paused in front of the new Plumas County courthouse and peered up at the dark, ominous-looking storm clouds rolling in over the mountains northwest of town. He frowned at the prospect of the approaching storm, well aware of the problems a heavy snowfall would bring.

It wasn't the thought of the cold or the inconvenience that bothered him, for those were things he could deal with. But other, more important problems accompanying snowstorms were less easily overcome. He knew, for instance, that a bad storm would drive deer down from the ridges to the lower valleys—valleys that would provide protection from wind and cold, but would concentrate the animals within easy reach of game poachers. If this happened, Mercer's problem would be one of investing time at the places he figured the poachers would most likely strike. There were many such potential trouble spots to choose from, and warden work under such circumstances could become a highly frustrating guessing game.

Mulling these thoughts over in his mind, Mercer turned and started down the main street of town. Near his car, he encountered a tall, sallow-faced individual by the name of George Crowder, a rancher in the Genesee Valley, some twenty miles north of Quincy. The man had large, deep-set eyes and the odd habit of blinking them often—slow, deliberate blinks—as though he were trying to clear his vision. He reminded Mercer of an owl.

It was something of a coincidence that Crowder should show up at that exact moment, for had Mercer been pressed to compose a list of poachers most likely to exploit the coming storm, Crowder would have been near the top of the list. Mercer had no doubts that Crowder, if snowed in and out of reach of the law, would likely take advantage of the situation and kill a deer or two. After returning Crowder's greeting, Mercer took the opportunity to warn the man.

"George, this storm is gonna drive some deer down onto your ranch," he said. "You'd best leave them alone."

Crowder blinked his eyes several times and assumed an expression of mild outrage. "Are you sayin' I'm a deer poacher?" he asked.

"Just call it a friendly warning," replied Mercer, climbing into his car.

*   *   *

It snowed hard all that night, and the following morning found the Quincy area under a foot and a half of new snow. But the storm had nearly passed, and patches of blue sky were showing through the clouds. It promised to be a clear but chilly day.

Mercer awoke that morning with a thought running through his mind; it was just a hunch, but he had learned to trust his hunches. Some instinct was telling him that George Crowder would ignore the warning given the previous day and kill a deer anyway, possibly just to say he had done it. So, while the sun was still low to the southeast, Mercer strapped his snowshoes onto his old Ford and headed for the Genesee Valley.

He made it only a short way past Taylorsville before the deep snow forced him to park the Ford. He proceeded then on his snowshoes, shuffling steadily up the valley along Indian Creek. He was headed toward Crowder's farm near the mouth of Red Clover Creek, some eight miles distant.

Now, Mercer's snowshoes weren't the traditional kind with rawhide webbing and wooden frames. "Webs," as they were known, had their place, but the snowshoes on which Mercer had become expert were actually the forerunners of our modern snow skis. They were thin, fourteen-foot-long, straight-grained Douglas fir boards turned up at one end. Known as 'long-shoes,' they had no foot harnesses, but were equipped with leather toe holders and wooden heel blocks.

As a standard accessory to his pair of long-shoes, Mercer carried a single four-foot-long wooden pole with a knob on one end. This he used simply as a brake for downhill travel. He would grasp the pole with both hands and straddle it, with the knob to the rear, when he went into his crouch for a downhill run. If it became necessary to slow his descent, he could thrust the knob end of the pole into the snow between the long-shoes, thus controlling his speed. For uphill travel, he would slip 'socks' made of mattress ticking onto the rear half of each ski. Thus equipped, and by means of an odd, shuffling gait, he could negotiate a fairly substantial grade. For lesser grades, a turn or two of light rope around each ski would do the job.

Mercer had been taught the secrets of long-shoe skiing by Albert Gould, a forest ranger in La Porte. Gould had once been a mail carrier charged with the formidable task of delivering the winter mail between La Porte and Quincy. This he had accomplished through the use of long-shoe skis. He had toiled through the arduous round trip several times a month, packing the heavy mail sacks over miles of snowbound trails. His exploits had become legendary.

Mercer, with Gould's help, had mastered long-shoe

skiing, and he patrolled by this means during his first six winters as a warden. Game violators in Plumas and Sierra counties soon learned they were never safe from Mercer, who was apt to turn up in any place, at any time, even in the dead of winter.

And so it was, that winter morning, that Mercer set out on his long-shoes up the Genesee Valley, following his hunch. Sweet-smelling wood smoke rose from the chimneys of the few farmhouses he passed, and he gave these infrequent dwellings a wide berth as he continued up the valley. As he trudged along, with the countryside muffled in its new blanket of snow, a dull silence prevailed—a silence broken only occasionally by the lowing of cattle or the sharp ring of an axe. Upon nearing Crowder's farm, Mercer moved into the trees along the creek so as to be less visible. The valley had by then narrowed to more of a canyon.

Continuing on a short distance, he encountered fresh tracks in the snow. A deer had passed through sometime within the last hour. Then he stopped abruptly, studying the snow up ahead. He could see where the deer tracks had been joined by those of a man, and it took no great tracking skill to see that the man had been trailing the deer. Mercer's pulse quickened as he took up the trail himself, senses alert.

Suddenly, a rifle shot exploded up ahead, sounding incredibly loud in the canyon. Fine, powdery snow sifted down from the fir trees as the echo of the shot rebounded from the canyon walls. Mercer slipped out of his long-shoes and continued silently on foot, stepping carefully in the tracks made by the poacher.

He had gone no more than a hundred yards when the forest opened into a small meadow. There, on the far side of the clearing, was George Crowder, kneeling in the snow, knife in hand, beside the body of a freshly killed doe. The man's sleeves were rolled up to the elbows, his forearms crimson with fresh blood as he went about the business of field dressing the deer. Wisps of steam rose from the warm carcass of the animal as he worked.

Mercer crept to within twenty feet of the man before he was detected. Upon hearing the soft crunch of snow behind him, Crowder whirled around and stood up, eyes blinking furiously. At the sight of Mercer, his knees went weak and he nearly collapsed in the snow. But he managed to stay on his feet, trembling, with an incredulous look on his face.

"I warned you, George," said Mercer. "I told you not to do it."

"Mercer!" said Crowder, gasping for breath. "How did you . . . how did you get in here?"

When Mercer replied that he had come in on foot, Crowder just stared at the ground and shook his head in disbelief.

There was no possibility of getting Crowder to jail that day, so Mercer had no choice but to issue a citation and instruct Crowder to contact Judge McCutcheon at the Greenville Justice Court when the roads were passable.

"I just don't see how you did it," said Crowder, as he signed the citation and handed the book back to Mercer.

His business with Crowder finished, Mercer started back down the valley, dragging the doe behind him on a short piece of rope. Crowder offered to help, but Mercer declined, electing to handle the task himself. Crowder, blinking his owl eyes in dismay, watched until the warden was out of sight, then turned and trudged back toward his cabin. Mercer paused only long enough to step into his long-shoes, then continued on his way.

It was a grueling eight-mile struggle, and sunset found the warden still several miles from his truck. With darkness closing in, and with his strength failing, he was forced to quarter the deer and leave most of it in a tree, packing only one hind quarter back to his car. As it was, he arrived long after dark, totally spent, but well satisfied with his day's work.

It was about five weeks before the road to Greenville was open and Crowder had his day in court. Judge

McCutcheon, upon learning that Mercer had warned
the man the day before the violation, hammered him
for five hundred dollars, which was the heaviest fine
Mercer had heard of to that date for a deer case.

*   *   *

Mercer suffered a very close call on his long-shoes
one frigid morning near Taylor Creek, east of Quincy.
Losing control on a steep downslope, he ricocheted off
some trees and took a crushing fall, which left him
unconscious in the snow. He must have remained there
for a considerable time, for when he finally awoke, he
was dangerously weak and numb with cold. It took all
his strength to crawl back to his truck. It was a serious
accident that nearly cost him his life, and the experience
had a pronounced dampening effect on his zeal for
snowshoeing.

Stakeout at Trumbly's Still

Grover Trumbly grimaced as the harsh liquid he called 'jackass' burned a trail down his abused throat.

"Not bad," he said, smacking his lips.

With watering eyes, he peered around at what resembled the hidden laboratory of some mad scientist. Huge wooden vats and strange-looking kettles connected with yards of coiled copper tubing were arranged in the spacious hollow dug into the mountainside. The whole thing was roofed over with corrugated metal. A fire burned beneath one of the vessels containing a hot, bubbling liquid, and the air was heavy with the pungent, sour aroma of fermenting grain.

Satisfied that his crude distillery was functioning properly, Trumbly grabbed his .30-30 rifle and stalked out into the evening. The sun had already disappeared behind the mountains to the west and the shadows were darkening as he made his way silently up the trail behind his still. A gentle breeze, fragrant with the sweet smell of high-desert sage, drifted up from the level plain below.

The buck was there on the ridge where Trumbly expected it to be—where he had seen it the last two nights. It stood facing him, motionless with ears erect, antlers silhouetted against the darkening sky. Trumbly thumbed back the hammer of his old rifle, then paused to look around. It wouldn't do to have an audience. But there was no one to be seen in the sage-flats below. All was quiet, as it always was. And when he raised the rifle and found the buck in his sights, he was absolutely certain that he was the only human being for ten miles in any direction.

He was wrong. Not quite a mile to the south, at the ruins of an old cabin on the same ridge, two vigilant game wardens were about to partake of a typical game warden dinner. Warden Oscar Shoemaker opened a box of soda crackers, while Warden Gene Mercer rolled back the lid on a can of sardines. Mercer was about to spear one of the oily little fish with his pocketknife, when the sharp sound of a rifle shot brought him up short.

Both wardens swiveled to face north, where the echo of the shot still reverberated through the canyons. It was the shot they had been expecting—and hoping for—yet it still caught them by surprise.

"That's gotta be him," said Mercer, peering off toward Trumbly's still, which, due to the contour of the ridge, was just out of sight. Shoemaker reached for a battered pair of binoculars and scanned the area for a full minute.

"Well, he's not out where I can see him," he said. "But you can bet he got a deer."

"What do you wanna do?" asked Mercer, turning to face the more experienced warden.

"Well, I'm tempted to head over there," said Shoemaker, "but the country's too open. There's too good a chance he'll see us coming . . . and if he puts some distance between him and the deer, we won't have a case."

"We could crawl up on him tonight," said Mercer, "but I doubt he'd have the deer at his shack. He's too smart for that. But he'll be takin' it with him when he goes to town. I think we should wait him out."

"I agree," said Shoemaker. "Let's wait and catch him with it in his car."

With that settled, the two wardens sat down and resumed their dinner.

*   *   *

The year was 1930 and times were hard. The Great Depression had put thousands of Americans out of work, and Prohibition was denying them the means to drown their sorrows. It wasn't surprising that many turned to distilling their own liquor, and a lucrative black market for potent homemade whiskey had been born.

To counter this problem, the federal government appointed federal prohibition officers to deal with it. Know as prohi's (pronounced pro-highs), the prohibition officers were stationed strategically around the state to ferret out illegal bootleggers.

The hills were full of bootleggers, and, as could be expected, the game wardens stumbled onto them frequently. This brought up the problem of what to do with them. Since bootleggers were lawbreakers, Mercer's natural instinct was to arrest them, but he soon found that when he did so, he got no support from the prohi's. In fact, the prohi's seemed to resent his getting involved. In time he found out, to his disgust, that most of the prohi's in his area were corrupt and were accepting payoffs in one form or another.

But it was the attitude of the people that convinced Mercer to ignore the problem of bootleggers. Prohibition was unpopular with the people, and had Mercer chosen to make an issue of it, it would have cost him public support and hindered his efforts to protect wildlife. He therefore let it be known that he would be no threat to bootleggers, as long as they obeyed the Fish and Game laws.

In time, he came to know many of the bootleggers in his area, and became friends with most of them. When they learned to trust him, they became good sources of information that resulted in the arrests of many troublesome poachers. He found also that the hidden stills, particularly during the winter, provided snug hideouts from which to watch problem areas of his district. He therefore spent countless hours warming himself by fires that heated distilling equipment, listening for shots, and watching the mountain roads for poachers. During this time, he also became something of an authority on distilling techniques.

While most of the bootleggers were otherwise law-abiding citizens, not all of them obeyed the game laws, and Mercer was quick to come down on the crooked ones. Such was the case with Grover Trumbly. Mercer had received word that not only was Trumbly selling whiskey, but he was selling deer meat as well. It was this information that sent Mercer and Shoemaker to the lonely ridge on the eastern slopes of the Sierras, to stay in the old cabin and wait for Grover Trumbly to kill his next deer.

The wardens arrived at the cabin in the morning, and Grover Trumbly obligingly poached a deer in the early evening of that same day—a fine piece of luck for the wardens. But now they would have to wait until Trumbly made his periodic trip to Susanville, which meant anything from a two-hour to a two-day wait. Waiting was part of the job, however, and the two wardens gave it little thought.

*   *   *

Since there was a chance that Trumbly would make his run to town during the night, Mercer and Shoemaker spent the chilly night taking turns, one sleeping while the other watched the road. But dawn found the situation unchanged from the night before.

Mercer sat huddled in his blanket, looking eastward into Nevada, watching the sun begin its slow ascent into the winter sky. He longed for a hot cup of coffee to ward off the cold, but that was out of the question. There would be no coffee this frigid morning, for as close as they were to Trumbly's still, they couldn't risk a fire.

Mercer reached for his canteen and was about to take a drink when suddenly he stopped. Had he heard something? He cocked his head and listened. There it was again, the faint sound of an engine. A car was coming. But it couldn't be Trumbly, for it was coming from the wrong direction. Throwing his blanket aside, he stood and walked quickly to where he had a view of the road leading up from the sage flats below. There it was, an old car winding its way up toward the cabin.

Shoemaker, curled up in his bedroll, responded instantly to Mercer's low whistle.

"There's a car coming, Shoe," said Mercer. "Looks like it's comin' up here."

"Damn," muttered Shoemaker. "That ain't good."

Since the cabin was perched on a high bench near the top of the ridge, the two men in the old car were unable to see that the place was occupied until they arrived. When the cabin came into view, they were alarmed to see two stern-faced men waiting for them.

"State game wardens," said Shoemaker, approaching the driver and displaying his badge. Mercer approached the passenger side of the vehicle and did the same.

Mercer immediately recognized the two men as Washoe Indians from the reservation at Pyramid Lake, across the Nevada border. It was well known among the wardens that the Washoes liked to sneak across into California now and then to pop off a deer—which was undoubtedly what these two had in mind. They had a rifle with them, and they were highly nervous to be in the presence of two California wardens.

The arrival of the Indians posed a serious problem for the wardens: They knew that Trumbly was aquainted with some of the Washoes, and if the two Indians were allowed to leave, there was a good chance that Trumbly would be warned of his peril. But Shoemaker solved the problem when he produced a heavy pair of handcuffs.

"Sorry, men, but you're going to have to stick around for a while," he said, as he handcuffed the two Indians together, right wrist to right wrist.

The Indians begged and pleaded, promising to head straight for the reservation if they could be released, but it was to no avail. The wardens escorted them into the cabin where they were instructed to sit and remain quiet.

The day passed slowly with no apparent activity in the direction of Trumbly's still, and when night came, the wardens traded off again with the watch. The Indians complained bitterly, particularly when it got chilly. Not equipped for an all-night stay, they suffered terribly from the cold. It was only after considerable begging and teeth-chattering on their part that the wardens relented and allowed them to build a small fire.

Morning again found the situation unchanged, and it wasn't until late afternoon that Trumbly made his move.

"Here he comes," said Mercer excitedly, as the bootlegger's car appeared in the distance.

After a quick look, Shoemaker dug out his handcuff key and hurriedly released the two Indians.

"Stay here for another ten minutes, then you can leave," he instructed. "But if we ever catch you here again, comin' over here to hunt, we're gonna put you in jail."

"You can bet *we* won't be back," one of them replied, rubbing the red welt on his wrist.

*   *   *

Grover Trumbly, in his old Chevrolet touring car, was motoring along at a good clip, enjoying the afternoon, when suddenly he spotted another vehicle bearing down on him from the west. Instinctively, he knew he was in trouble. He considered making a run for it, but he discarded the idea, aware that he wouldn't be able to outrun anything in his old car. His only chance was to use his head and try to talk his way out of it.

The other vehicle reached the main road ahead of him, and Trumbly wasn't surprised when it pulled crossways in the road, blocking his path. He pulled to a stop a few feet from the other vehicle, his heart pounding.

"State game wardens," said Mercer as he and Shoemaker approached Trumbly's vehicle. "Where are you going in such a hurry?"

"Just on my way to town," replied Trumbly. "Wardens, huh? How 'bout a taste of my merchandise?" he asked, forcing a smile and holding up a gallon jug of his fresh-run corn whiskey.

"To tell you the truth, Mr. Trumbly, we're more interested in what you've got in the back," said Mercer, and Trumbly's smile vanished.

The wardens found the deer, quartered and wrapped in flour sacks, hidden beneath an old tarp in the back, along with several gallon jugs of illegal whiskey. At this point, Trumbly lost his temper and became verbally abusive with the two wardens. This was a mistake, for, suddenly, he found himself wearing Shoemaker's handcuffs. Trussed up and helpless in the patrol car, he completed his ride to Susanville with Shoemaker, who drove him straight to the county jail.

Mercer drove Trumbly's car into town and went directly to the federal offices. There—under his watchful eye—the prohibition officers reluctantly took possession of Trumbly's jackass whiskey and prepared charges against him for bootlegging.

Trumbly was ultimately convicted of bootlegging and deer poaching and was sentenced to a stay in the county jail. Following his release, he soon drifted back into his bootlegging habits again, but when it came to deer poaching, he was permanently reformed.

A Dangerous Enemy

Frank Marizanni could easily have passed for a Mafia boss, for he certainly looked and acted the part. There was something sinister in his appearance and imposing personality, a distinct aura of strength and power that intimidated other men. Born to control, he was a ruthless manipulator of people—a user, a man accustomed to having things *his* way.

He considered himself a businessman, but, in fact, he was something of a racketeer. Not only was he heavily into bootlegging, with his own stills operated by his own men, but he maintained a string of brothels near the lumber camps of Sierra and Plumas counties. In addition, he owned the Beckwourth Lodge.

From the street, the Beckwourth Lodge appeared to be a hotel, but in reality it was a bar that catered to the wealthy and openly served Marizanni's own locally produced whiskey. The only such establishment for miles around, it was a highly popular hangout for those who enjoyed hard liquor and disapproved of Prohibition. Its patrons included some important people in the area, not the least of whom was Edwin Thorpe, the head federal prohibition officer himself.

But Warden Gene Mercer was neither impressed nor

intimidated. He considered Marizanni a crook, and when he received information that the man had been killing deer out of season, he set out at once to investigate. According to the informant, Marizanni had been killing deer and taking them to his home in Portola. The informant went on to say that Marizanni had at least one deer at his home that very minute.

The following morning, armed with a search warrant, Mercer arrived at Marizanni's door.

"Mercer, what are you doin' here?" demanded Marizanni, staring out through his doorway at the warden.

"I'm here on business," said Mercer. "I understand you've been killin' deer."

"That's nonsense," said Marizanni. "Who told you that?"

Marizanni, accustomed to the fact that he was feared by most lawmen in the county, was both surprised and enraged that Mercer would have the audacity to brace him at his home over something as minor as deer poaching.

"Mr. Marizanni, I have a search warrant here. I'm afraid I'm going to have to search your house," said Mercer, displaying the document signed that morning by a reluctant judge.

Marizanni grabbed the warrant and scanned through it, his teeth clenched in anger.

"Now if you'll stand aside, sir, I'm coming in," said Mercer, taking a step forward. Marizanni hesitated a moment, but then, seeing the look of determination and total confidence in the warden's eyes, he stepped back, sensing that he was facing no ordinary man.

Mercer walked in and began his search, going from room to room. He was puzzled at first, for a search of the usual storage places for fresh meat turned up nothing. In a shed behind the house, he found fresh blood and deer hair, but no meat. Then, as he stood pondering the situation, he spotted two covered wooden barrels in one corner of the shed. Upon lifting the lid on one of the barrels, he found it to contain a wine-colored liquid smelling strongly of garlic. Submerged in this spicy solution were large chunks of meat which he was certain were venison.

Marizanni gritted his teeth in barely controlled rage as Mercer rolled up one sleeve and fished the meat out of the barrels, piece by piece, enough meat, Mercer estimated, to have come from at least two deer. He packed up his pickled evidence, more than eighty pounds of it, and carried it out to his car.

"Mercer, I'll have your job for this," threatened Marizanni as the warden left the house. But Mercer didn't even bother to look back. He drove away, leaving Marizanni standing on the front porch, glaring after him, seething with anger.

*   *   *

Before charges could be filed against Marizanni, Mercer knew that the meat would have to be positively identified by experts at a laboratory. He therefore sent off a sample to the University of California's Strawberry Canyon Lab for testing. Several weeks later, to his dismay, the tests came back inconclusive. The fact that the meat was permeated with wine and garlic had somehow adversely affected the tests. Mercer was thoroughly disgusted.

Marizanni, upon hearing the news, immediately demanded the return of his meat. Mercer had no choice but to comply. He did, however, take some grim satisfaction in the fact that the meat chunks, which he had stored hanging in his woodshed, had shrunken and dried to the consistency of oak stobs. Marizanni was again outraged, threatening to sue Mercer and the state of California. These were empty threats, however, for he never followed through. But one thing was certain: Mercer had made a dangerous enemy—a vindictive enemy who would _never_ forget.

A Brush with the Head Fed

Mercer had learned, soon after his arrival in Portola, that Edwin Thorpe, the head federal prohibition officer in the area, was crooked. It was well known that Thorpe, a tall, heavyset man of middle age, with the smooth look of a politician, was not only taking payoffs from bootleggers, but was a regular patron of Marizanni's Beckwourth Lodge as well. There were also tales of him killing an occasional out-of-season deer—rumors which Mercer sensed were more fact than fiction. While Mercer had never actually met the man, he knew him by reputation and felt that he was worth keeping an eye on.

One summer afternoon, shortly before dusk, Mercer spotted Thorpe in Chilcoot. Thorpe was driving north out of the little town, headed into the same mountainous area where, a few years earlier, Mercer had tangled with the doctor from Reno. It was an area thick with deer, and Mercer, immediately suspicious, set out to follow the man.

Mercer kept Thorpe's dust trail in sight as long as he could, but when the road entered the mountains, he chose a high spot to wait and listen. To continue on would have been to risk blundering onto Thorpe too soon. And besides, he reasoned, if Thorpe intended to poach a deer, it wouldn't take him long to find one, and he would probably bring the animal out the same way he went in. So, as night approached, Mercer settled down to wait—something at which he had become quite good.

*   *   *

Edwin Thorpe slipped the new scoped rifle from its tooled leather case. He delighted again in the pleasing combination of blue-black metal and polished walnut, and the pleasant smell of linseed oil and solvent. A recent gift from Frank Marizanni, the precision weapon had arrived shortly after Thorpe had ordered his prohibition officers to stay clear of Portola—the center of Marizanni's bootlegging operation.

Directing the rifle's muzzle out the left window of his car, Thorpe operated the bolt, ramming a shiny brass cartridge into the firing chamber. Shouldering the weapon and squinting through the telescope sight, he centered the cross hairs on the chest of a three-point buck, the largest of several deer browsing some two hundred yards away at the far edge of a grassy meadow. He squeezed the trigger and the rifle boomed, the recoil like a punch to his shoulder. The buck staggered, then lurched toward the forest, managing forty yards before it collapsed.

Thorpe had seen many deer that evening, but he had chosen the three-point simply because it was close to the road. After replacing the rifle in its case, he drove across the meadow and hid his car in the trees, only a few yards from the deer. He then produced a Case four-inch folding knife and a canteen of water and went to work on the animal. A half hour later, he had the deer field dressed, loaded into his car, and covered with an old tarp. He washed his hands and his knife thoroughly with water from the canteen, then climbed into the car and started back toward Chilcoot.

It was still light enough to see when he rounded a bend and found the road blocked by another vehicle. There, to his horror, stood Warden Gene Mercer. Now, Thorpe only knew Mercer by sight and by reputation, but it was a formidable reputation. This was the man who had dared to pinch his friend Marizanni, the tough new warden who seldom slept and who seemed to be everywhere at once. This was the man everyone was talking about.

Thorpe silently cursed his bad luck as he applied the brakes, but even then his mind was formulating a plan. He hadn't arrived at his station in life by being slow-witted, and by the time his car came to he stop, he was ready. Jumping from the vehicle, he hurried forward to meet the warden.

"Aren't you the game warden?" he asked. Mercer answered to the affirmative and Thorpe continued.

"You're just the man I wanna see. I just passed a couple of guys loading a deer into a car about a mile and a half back. They were headed north, but if you hurry, I think you can catch 'em."

Thorpe held his breath, hoping desperately that Mercer would rush back to his car and head out. But it didn't happen.

"Aren't you Mr. Thorpe?" Mercer asked, noting the slight tremor in the other man's hands.

"That's right," answered Thorpe nervously, "I work for the federal government. I'm the head prohibition officer around here."

"Well, sir, what are you doing out here this evening?" asked Mercer, strolling casually toward Thorpe's car.

"Just out for a drive," Thorpe replied, as he tried to maneuver himself between his car and Mercer.

"Well, I'd like to have a quick look in your car, then I'll be on my way," said Mercer, stepping around Thorpe.

"Wait a minute," said Thorpe in his most authoritative voice, again stepping in front of Mercer. "This is government property, you can't look in here."

"You'd better stand aside, Mr. Thorpe. I'm investigating a possible violation, and it wouldn't do for you to interfere," said Mercer, looking the other man in the eyes.

There was no misunderstanding Mercer's hard gaze, and Thorpe knew that to resist further would do him no good. With a sigh, he sat down on his front bumper, taking the load off his shaking knees. Mercer looked in the car and immediately uncovered the deer.

"Mercer, do you know what you're doing to me?" asked Thorpe, bent forward, staring at the ground, his head in his hands. "This is going to cost me my job."

"Well, Mr. Thorpe," said Mercer, as he dragged the deer out of the car, "I know you've been doing this for a long time, and I wouldn't be doin' *my* job if I let you go."

Mercer loaded the deer into his own car, along with Thorpe's fancy rifle, then wrote the man a citation. Thorpe was silent through all of this, responding only when called upon by Mercer. After finishing his work, Mercer drove away, leaving Thorpe still sitting on the bumper of his car, staring at the ground.

*   *   *

As it happened, Thorpe didn't lose his job, but his appearance before a Sierra County judge embarrassed him severely and cost him his new rifle and a stiff fine. Mercer had made another dangerous enemy.

A few weeks later, Mercer got wind that Thorpe, while drinking one night at the Beckwourth Lodge, had announced to all present that he would pay five hundred dollars. to anyone who would do away with Mercer. Upon hearing this, Mercer went immediately to Captain Sanders, and that evening the two of them headed for the Beckwourth Lodge.

All activity in the barroom came to an immediate halt as Mercer, grim-faced and flanked by Captain Sanders, strode through the door. Mercer paused for a moment, his eyes adjusting to the dim light, searching the line of patrons at the bar and those seated at the several tables. All were staring at him. It was at a table near one corner that Mercer spotted Thorpe, seated with Marizanni. All eyes followed Mercer as he headed for the table.

"I heard you've put a price on my head," said Mercer, eyes narrowed, fixing Thorpe with a hostile gaze.

"Well, Mr. Mercer, you can't believe everything you hear," said Thorpe, shifting nervously, doing his best to return Mercer's stare.

"But I believe *this*," said Mercer, "and I'll tell you what ... I'm going to assume that you're intending to kill me if you get the chance, and I'm gonna act accordingly. The next time I run into you out there, I'm gonna start shootin' first, before *you* have the chance."

He then turned and stomped out, with Sanders close on his heels. The silence prevailed for a few seconds longer, then gave way to excited chatter.

A few days later, Mercer was cautiously approached by a very humble Edwin Thorpe, who apologized profusely, claiming that his comments regarding a price on Mercer's head were only in jest. Mercer, however, knew better, certain that Thorpe would hurt him if ever given the opportunity.

Summer Duties

Warden Gene Mercer knelt on the shore of Little Holly Lake, high in the Sierras, and pried the lid from the ten-gallon milk can he had packed on his back up the mountain. Peering inside, he noted with satisfaction that most of the five hundred rainbow trout fingerlings had survived the trip nicely and were busily milling around in a dense school beneath the chunks of floating ice.

He replaced the lid and gently shook the can back and forth to aerate the water, then immersed the lower half of the container into the clear, icy water of the lake. There it would remain to slowly 'temper,' or adjust, to the temperature of the lake, for it wouldn't do to subject the tiny fish to temperature shock.

He had picked up the ice-packed can of fingerlings that morning at the Sulphur Creek Hatchery and driven them to Gold Lake, where he rowed them across to the north shore. There, he carefully poured out half the water from the milk can, hoisted it onto his back, and started up the steep trail that would take him to Little Holly Lake. It was a grueling, mile-and-a-half climb that took nearly an hour, and when he arrived, he was soaked, front and back, from water that had sloshed from the can as he trudged along.

While waiting out the tempering process, Mercer peeled off his wet shirt, spread it on a granite boulder to dry, and looked around with deep appreciation. Little Holly Lake was beautiful, a fine example of the picturesque alpine lakes hidden here and there at higher elevations of the Sierras. Nestled in a boulder-strewn valley and flanked by sparse stands of firs and white pines, it lay in total calm, its unblemished surface a perfect mirror reflecting the blue summer sky and the rugged image of the granite cliffs that towered above.

But like many such lakes at that time, Little Holly was barren—it contained no fish. While its banks and bottom were rich with insect life, and its crystalline waters the perfect environment for trout, there were absolutely none. And this was the reason for Mercer's visit. When he judged that the time was right, he gently inverted the milk can and emptied its precious contents into the lake—and with something akin to paternal pride, he watched as the tiny trout explored their new home.

The following day, there were more trout to plant in another alpine lake, and more the day after that—for it was summer, and summer was the time for planting fish.

The transporting and planting of trout was a highly time-consuming activity, and during the thirties and forties the responsibility was almost entirely that of the wardens. While the Fish and Game Division staffed hatcheries all over the state to raise millions of fingerling trout each year, there were no crews on the payroll to plant them. It was the warden force that handled the job, and mountain wardens in particular could expect to spend most of their time during the summer months planting fish. Only the weekends remained for patrol work.

Mercer worked mainly out of the trout hatchery at Sulphur Creek in Plumas County, a typical operation of the thirties and forties. In the early mornings, he would go to the hatchery and load the well-iced ten-gallon milk cans containing fingerling trout onto a vehicle known as a flatbed Dodge Graham. The cans were arranged on the truck in columns such that a walkway was left down the center. This allowed a man equipped with an aerating device to periodically walk between the columns of milk cans and aerate the water. The aerating device was simply a large tin can pierced with large holes and attached to a handle. The 'aerator man' would grasp the handle and vigorously thrust the can in and out of the water in each milk can, thus creating a turbulence that would provide fresh oxygen for the fish.

While on the road, aeration of the fish cans was no problem, for driving the poor roads of that time usually provided plenty of agitation to keep the water well oxygenated. But when traveling the better roads, the driver would go out of his way to hit every available chuckhole.

When lakes and streams scheduled for planting were not accessible by road, the fish were packed in by horse or mule, or quite often on the backs of the wardens. Mercer took this work seriously, and he was responsible for the first introductions of trout into many high-country lakes and streams. In fact, he hiked long miles out of his way to locate new waters in which to plant trout. It was not uncommon at that time for a stream to have a thriving population of trout downstream from a waterfall, while above the waterfall it could be totally devoid of fish. It was Mercer who first stocked many of these barren sections of streams, more than half a century ago.

*   *   *

At various times during his career, Mercer, like all wardens, was called upon to do something different. It has always been the case in Fish and Game work that when odd jobs arise, they are delegated to the nearest warden. Whether it's the collection of bobcat jaws or bear teeth or whatever, the warden often gets stuck with the job. Such was the case when, in the mid-thirties, Mercer was called upon to collect rabbits.

At that time, in Sierra County and surrounding areas, there was an outbreak of the disease tularemia, or 'rabbit fever,' as it is known. While the disease normally infects rabbits, humans are susceptible as well, and in humans, tularemia often proves fatal.

When the outbreak occurred in Mercer's patrol district, and when researchers needed rabbits for study purposes, they naturally called on Mercer to take the risks and do the collecting. Therefore, for more than four months, he collected forty rabbits per week, with a .22 rifle, and sent them to University of California pathologists for examination.

Another odd assignment required him to collect pelicans. There had been complaints from some politically important citizens that the large, white, inland pelicans from Pyramid Lake, Nevada, were eating trout in the Sierra Valley. Mercer, to his disgust, received orders to shoot several of the big birds to see if they had been eating trout. Mercer argued that they had been eating trout for thousands of years, but the orders stood. He therefore gritted his teeth and popped off a couple. Sure enough, they had been eating trout. He submitted his report, and nothing else ever came of the matter.

*   *   *

In March of 1931, Mercer was transferred to the Quincy patrol district. Two major construction projects were underway in the Quincy area at that time. The Western Pacific Railroad was building a new line from Keddie to New Beiber, and, at the same time, large crews consisting of mainly convict labor were heavily engaged on the steep canyon walls of the Feather River Canyon, blasting and hacking out the route that was to become the new Highway 70. Mercer's captain felt that the influx of the hundreds of construction workers posed a threat to wildlife, and he therefore wanted a good warden in the area.

The new district offered Mercer not only a change of scenery, but a nicer environment for his wife and daughter. His wife, Edna, had grown tired of the primitive mud streets and board sidewalks of Portola, not to mention the brothels and the multitudes of rowdy lumberjacks.

Soon after getting settled in Quincy, Mercer rode a freight train down the Feather River Canyon to Oroville, where a brand-new Model B Ford pickup awaited him. The Division of Fish and Game had finally decided to equip its wardens with state patrol vehicles. Mercer was in high spirits that afternoon, as he drove his new truck up the rough and winding Oroville Quincy Road, back to Quincy and his new patrol district.

He wasted no time in outfitting his new truck. He installed a siren given to him by his friend Oscar Schumacker, and for a red light, he used a red handkerchief tied over a white spotlight—he found that it worked surprisingly well. He then added his grub box, his bedroll, and his brass field glasses, and he was ready to go to work.

Also, at about this time he acquired another side-arm—one that was more appropriate for duty use than the fancy, pearl-handled Smith & Wesson. He purchased a .38-caliber Colt 6″ Shooting Master revolver equipped with a 'cockeyed hammer' and a King gold bead front sight. A Plumas County deputy sheriff then made him a pair of custom grips from a nice piece of black willow. He now had a pistol to be proud of.

A Lesson in Attention

Warden Gene Mercer applied the brakes, bringing his Ford patrol car to an abrupt halt. Peering back, his head out the side window, he backed up, examining the ground at the edge of the roadway. Something had caught his eye. There it was, the fresh, telltale marks left by the tires of a motorcycle leaving the road. The informant had been right. Mercer shifted to first gear and started forward again. It wouldn't do to linger—at least not yet.

Continuing down the road, he drove nearly a half mile before turning off to park in a stand of pines. Then, grabbing his binoculars and citation book, he started back on foot. Not far below the road, down a gentle slope, Bucks Lake lay shimmering in the early morning sun. Mercer studied the shoreline as he walked along. He could clearly see the buoys that marked the fishing closure intended to protect the spring-spawning rainbows. The spawners were now congregated near the mouth of Bucks Creek, tempting bait for poachers. But the shoreline appeared deserted.

Arriving at the tire prints, Mercer followed them down the slope into the forest. He hadn't gone far when he saw it, leaning against a pine—a shiny new Indian motorcycle. He approached the machine and carefully touched one of its two cylinders with his hand. It was still warm.

Heading back up the slope, Mercer hiked to the top of a granite outcropping from which he could again see the lake a quarter mile below. Leaning across a gray boulder, he scanned the shoreline with his binoculars. As the mouth of Bucks Creek swung through his circular field of view, he stopped and readjusted the focus. Sure enough, he had detected movement in the willows at the water's edge. Every few seconds an arm bearing a fishing rod was visible through the foliage. Mercer slipped down from the boulder and began a stealthy approach.

*   *   *

Francis Coito whipped his cane rod toward the lake, released the spool on his ancient 'thumb burner' reel, and managed a twenty-foot cast. The hooked night crawler and cork float hit the water with a light splash. The cork had barely settled when suddenly it bobbed once and disappeared. Coito reared back, setting the hook on a two-pound rainbow. The fish broke water twice, twisting and thrashing like a small marlin, then flashed away in a series of powerful runs. Coito played the fish expertly, and after a three-minute battle he dragged it, spent and beaten, onto the bank. After taking a few seconds to look around, satisfied he was still alone, he strung the fish on a stringer with four other nice trout.

People who knew Francis Coito found it strange that he held such a passion for fishing, such a tranquil pursuit, for he was known to be a violent man by nature. In fact, he had few friends due to his volatile temper and his tendency to fight at the least provocation.

But Coito *did* enjoy fishing, particularly illegal fishing, for he enjoyed the element of risk. He took great delight in sneaking into closed lakes and streams and ignoring limits and fishing seasons. But he wasn't stupid. He took precautions to avoid being caught, even going so far as to use a motorcycle for his illegal forays. He found that the machine would go most anywhere, yet it was easy to conceal.

In short, Francis Coito—with his love for illegal fishing and his lethal temper—was the perfect time bomb waiting to explode in the face of a warden. It was inevitable that he tangle with the law in some violent confrontation, and that confrontation was to occur this spring morning at Bucks Lake in 1934.

Mercer had watched through a veil of pine boughs, thirty feet away, as Coito caught his last trout, and he'd remained motionless as the man warily looked around. But now, with Coito kneeling and facing away, intent on skewering another fat night crawler with his hook, Mercer made his move. Slipping silently from behind the stand of young pines, he eased his way to within ten feet of the unsuspecting violator.

"Good morning, sir," said Mercer, and Coito whirled around, spilling his can of worms.

"Looks like you've done pretty well," continued the warden, eyeing the stringered trout lying in the shallow water, gills pulsing weakly. Coito remained silent, still in shock.

"I'm a state game warden," said Mercer, pulling his vest aside and revealing the badge pinned to his flannel shirt. "Of course you know this area's closed to fishing . . . I'll need to see your driver's license and your fishing license."

Coito hesitated, then pulled out his wallet and produced both licenses.

Mercer examined both documents, then began filling out a citation. Coito watched in silence, studying the warden—estimating his strengths, and alert for signs of weakness. He judged he had at least a two-inch height advantage over the warden and outweighed him by at least thirty pounds.

When Mercer finished writing and began the task

of explaining the citation, Coito wasn't listening. He was intent instead on looking for the right opportunity, measuring his chances. Then Mercer held out the citation book for the man's signature.

The punch caught Mercer square on the jaw. He saw it coming, a swift, roundhouse right, but not in time to react. There was just one sickening split second of realization before the jarring impact sent his thoughts spinning into darkness.

Mercer hit the ground hard, but even then his head was beginning to clear. He instinctively rolled to his knees and tried to get up. Even in his semiconscious state, he was aware that he was in serious trouble. More than one warden in the past had been knocked unconscious by a violator and then shot with his own gun or drowned.

The second punch came when he was still on all fours, but this time he partially deflected it. He felt a solid thump as the punch glanced off his skull, but it did little damage. His brain had started to function again, and although the second punch hadn't hurt him, he feigned injury, rolling to the ground and acting as though he couldn't get up.

When Coito, now confident of victory, came in to finish him with a kick to the face, Mercer was ready for him. On his knees again, he gathered his strength and at the last instant launched himself at his attacker, driving his head into the man's midsection. Coito cried out in surprise as he went down, the wind driven from his lungs. Mercer was on him then, furious and full of fight, and with a series of sharp blows, he methodically hammered the man senseless.

*   *   *

Later that day, when the battered violator was behind bars—a bandage protecting his shattered nose—Mercer gingerly examined his own badly bruised jaw and was reminded again of the grim fact that mistakes in his line of work could be extremely hazardous.

Hard Times

During the years of the Great Depression, an interesting phenomenon occurred in California. Thousands of desperate men abandoned the shanty-towns and breadlines of the cities to try their luck mining in gold country. There was, in fact, something of a second gold rush in the Sierras. With gold at about twenty dollars an ounce, it was possible for an industrious man with a shovel, a sluice box, and a little luck to eke out a living for himself and his family.

Since the Quincy patrol district encompassed some of the richest gold country in the state, it saw more than its share of miners. Their tents and lean-to shacks were everywhere along the banks of the rivers and streams. Ground that had been worked first by the forty-niners, then again by the Chinese, grudgingly yielded a bit more gold, and many hard-working miners were able to scrape by. But other gold miners were not so lucky. The valuable metal somehow eluded them, and starvation was prevalent.

In the early thirties, the government initiated programs to help feed the hungry victims of the Depression. Food distribution centers were established in key places around the state, and Quincy was the site of one of these centers. Tons of food were given away there every month, but to the unfortunate miners in the remote camps, Quincy might just as well have been on the moon.

Ultimately, it was Mercer who came to their rescue. It pained him to witness the suffering of these haggard people, and he couldn't bear to ignore them. There was also the problem of the wildlife they were slaughtering for lack of other food. He therefore came up with a plan to deliver the badly needed government supplies to the remote camps.

From the Quincy distribution center, he would pick up loads of Red Cross flour, rice, beans, and sometimes Argentine corned beef, and during the course of his patrols he would distribute this food among the grateful miners. Whenever possible, he supplemented the government supplies with venison from highway- and railroad-killed deer, which he would pick up and dress out himself.

When deer meat and government supplies were scarce, he and a few of the wealthier Plumas County residents would pool their own funds to buy food for the miners. Ten dollars would buy a full ton of potatoes from farmers in the nearby Genesee Valley, and Mercer would distribute a load each time he went on patrol.

When the roads were too bad to get to the mines by vehicle, Mercer carried the supplies in on his back, fifty pounds at a time. During the winter months, he often had to strap on the heavy packs and ski in on his long-shoes.

Despite the help he provided the miners, Mercer always insisted that they obey the Fish and Game laws, even when they were desperate for food. Yet he was known to have purchased, from his own pocket, fishing licenses for various miners as an option to having to arrest them later for fishing without one.

He provided another vital service to the miners as well: Such was their trust in him that they prevailed upon him to transport and sell their gold for them at the bank in Portola, where it brought the best price. He would bring the proceeds back to them either in cash or supplies, whichever they preferred.

Through efforts such as these, Mercer made life a lot easier for a good many people during the hard times of the thirties. And when the long ordeal was finally over, there were many who owed their very lives to him.

*   *   *

Not only did Mercer feed hungry miners, but during the more severe winters, he took it upon himself to feed starving, snowbound deer. Armed with an axe, he would make his rounds to the various spots where the deer congregated and chop down fresh cedar boughs for them. The deer learned to look forward to his visits and would eagerly follow him around.

The Squirrel Creek Nugget

Neoma Elliot paused from her washing and smiled as she recognized Gene Mercer coming up the trail. Straightening up from her laundry tub, she brushed a stray wisp of honey-colored hair from her eyes and waved a greeting to the young warden. Although her hands were permanently red and irritated from continual contact with lye soap, and faint lines and creases near her eyes gave her a slightly haggard appearance, she was still a beautiful woman by any measure. She had survived her years in the mining camps much better than most miner's wives and had proven to be an excellent wife and mother.

The Elliots were always happy to see Mercer. His visits usually meant a decent meal for a change, plus he was always full of interesting news from the outside. Yes, times were tough, but Mercer had made things a little easier.

"Good morning, Mrs. Elliot," said Mercer. "How's the family?"

"Just fine, Mr. Mercer," she answered. "Won't you come in?"

As they entered the small, two-room cabin perched on a rise above Squirrel Creek, the three Elliot children greeted the warden enthusiastically, their eyes glued to the burlap sack he carried in one hand.

"I brought you a few things," he said, hoisting the sack onto the board table.

Neoma peered into the sack which contained a few pounds of beans, some potatoes, and two cans of corned beef. She then looked up and met Mercer's gaze.

"Thank you, Mr. Mercer," she said simply, but the look in her eyes contained more gratitude than words could have ever conveyed . . . and for such a reward, Mercer gladly would have carried the sack another hundred miles.

"I also brought Jim a little tobacco," said Mercer, holding up the small cloth pouch of Bull Durham.

"He'll be happy about that," said Neoma with a smile. "He's up on his claim, where he always is."

Leaving the cabin, Mercer took the well-worn trail that led to Jim Elliot's claim a quarter mile upstream on Squirrel Creek. He found the man down on his knees, busily jamming away with a steel bar, working out a deep crevice in the serpentine bedrock near the creek.

"Looks like you're hard at it," said Mercer as he approached.

"Hello, Gene. You're just in time . . . I'm about to find one the size of a potato," said Elliot, still jabbing into the crevice with his bar. Then he put the bar aside, thrust his hand into the crevice, and brought it out slowly, bearing something that to Mercer looked like a rust-colored rock. It was obviously quite heavy, and when Elliot turned it over Mercer saw a scar in it where it had been struck by the iron bar. The exposed metal beneath the rust-red surface was a deep, lustrous gold. It was indeed an enormous gold nugget about the size of a large potato.

With a dazed look in his eyes, Elliot held the nugget before him and exclaimed, "I'll be damned, there it is! I'm gonna buy Neoma a washing machine."

*   *   *

Elliot was an instant celebrity in gold country, and miners came from far and wide to gaze at the Squirrel Creek Nugget. When the clamor had subsided somewhat, Mercer helped Elliot ship the nugget to the San Francisco mint, where, with gold at $20.50 per troy ounce, it brought $1064.68, an awesome sum at the time.

It was several weeks before Mercer again had the chance to visit the Elliot's cabin on Squirrel Creek, and as he approached he first noticed new curtains in the windows. Then he heard the clatter of a small engine accompanied by an odd chunk, chunk, chunking sound. Puzzled, he walked to the rear of the cabin where he encountered Neoma poised over the source of all the noise, busily cranking wet clothes through the wringer of her new gasoline-powered washing machine.

Frenchy's Last Ride

Dawn had come. Warden Gene Mercer shifted to low gear as he started up a long mountain grade, the patrol car growling along through a foot of new snow. It was 1932. Plumas County lay frozen in the grip of an unusually cold winter, and America struggled in the midst of the Great Depression. Rounding a bend, the warden suddenly leaned forward, peering hard through the windshield at a lonely cabin on the hillside. It was Frenchy's cabin, and Mercer was worried. There was no smoke coming from the chimney, no signs of life. Something was wrong.

The old man known as Frenchy lived alone, preferring his quiet cabin to a place in town. He had become a friend to Mercer, the bond between them being a common dislike for game poachers, and he made certain that the warden was kept apprised of any wrongdoings in the area. In return, Mercer looked out for Frenchy, taking him to town now and then to buy supplies with the check that arrived each month from France. When he didn't have time to stop, Mercer would honk when he passed the cabin along what is now Highway 70, between Spring Garden and Sloat, and Frenchy would always come to the door and wave.

But Frenchy was nowhere to be seen this frigid morning, and there was no response when Mercer sounded his horn. Upon reaching a level spot, Mercer nosed his car off the road into a snowdrift and started back on foot. As he approached, he studied the cabin and his apprehension grew. It was obvious from the unblemished snow that no one had been in or out of the dwelling for at least two days.

"Maybe he's sick and in the hospital," thought Mercer. Frenchy was in his seventies and could well have been having some kind of health problem. But something told Mercer that this wasn't the case.

The warden waded through snow well above his knees as he approached Frenchy's front porch. He climbed the steps and knocked loudly. But there was no answer— only an eerie silence. He tried the door and found it locked. Walking to the rear of the cabin, he was alarmed to see the back door standing partly open, a narrow wedge of powdery snow extending through the doorway into the kitchen. Approaching the door, Mercer peered inside.

"Frenchy?" he called, not really expecting a response.

He walked in, noting with concern the dishes and partly eaten meal cluttering the table. "This isn't like Frenchy," he worried. He had to steel himself to check the bedroom, afraid of what he would find. Holding his breath, he stepped to the door and peeked in, but aside from some rude furnishing the room was empty. Returning to the kitchen, he placed his hand on the wood stove—it was ice cold.

He stood there for a while, looking around the room, searching for some clue that could explain the mystery. But there was none. Frenchy was simply gone, and he had apparently left in a hurry. Mercer could think of nothing to do at this point but return to Quincy and notify the sheriff.

As he pulled the back door shut and started down the hill to his car, he happened to notice the old outhouse sitting back in the trees, a stone's throw from the cabin. He hesitated, then turned and started toward it.

"It won't hurt to check," he thought, as he approached the tiny structure of weathered boards.

He hadn't really expected to find anything and was therefore unprepared when he pulled open the door and there sat Frenchy. Mercer recoiled in horror at the sight of the little man perched unceremoniously on the wooden seat, his pants bunched down around his ankles, frozen solid as a plank. His head was lolled over to one side, his mouth agape, and he stared out at Mercer through half-open, unseeing eyes. Mercer stood back, recovering from his shock, his breath coming in ragged gasps. Then, as he calmed himself, he stared at the dead man and contemplated the indignity of the situation. What a grim joke it was for Frenchy to cash in his chips while sitting on the john. Mercer felt a twinge of guilt as he noted to himself that the situation was not entirely without humor.

"When your number's up, your number's up," he thought, as he closed the outhouse door and started back to his car.

With the help of a phone-company lineman who tapped into the telephone lines, Mercer got a call through to Sheriff Braden in Quincy.

"Hello, sheriff? This is Mercer. Frenchy's dead. You better send the coroner out here."

It was well over an hour before the coroner and his assistant pulled up below the cabin.

Getting Frenchy out of the outhouse and packed down the hill was no easy task, but loading him into the coroner's vehicle proved even tougher. Due to the unhandy position to which Frenchy was solidly committed, they couldn't come up with a satisfactory way to fit him in. The problem was that the coroner's transport system was designed to accommodate only those among the deceased who could be arranged in a reclining position . . . and such was not the case with Frenchy.

When he was placed on his back, his legs and feet stuck up. And since his arms were frozen out away from his body, he didn't lie well on his side. They tried him face forward on knees and forehead, but quickly ruled out that position. Finally they stepped back to ponder the problem.

"Why don't we just prop him up in the front seat?" asked the coroner's assistant with a grin, turning to humor to ease the moment. The coroner smiled briefly at the thought, but then turned to face his assistant. The man's suggestion, though made in jest, was not without merit. Frenchy's rigid sitting position—he might as well have been carved from blue marble—was undeniably well suited to vehicular travel.

A short time later, the coroner's vehicle, with the coroner at the wheel and his assistant stretched out comfortably in the rear, was winding its way down the snowbound highway toward Quincy. To the casual observer, Frenchy easily might have passed for just another traveler—for he made his last ride to town sitting stiffly upright in the front seat, surveying the passing countryside with a vacant stare.

Saved by a Friend

When Mercer left the Portola patrol district, the vacancy was filled by a new warden, an ex-lumberjack by the name of Francis Fay Johnston. Now, Francis Fay was not fond of the first part of his name, preferring instead to go by the name Jack. And as he stood six feet, three inches and weighed upward of 220 pounds, he received few arguments on the subject. But despite his imposing appearance, Johnston was a good-natured, friendly individual and very easy to like. Mercer soon found him to be a good warden, extremely capable, and a good man to have with you in a bind.

One morning, while Mercer and Johnston were patrolling together up the Oroville Quincy Road in Johnston's Model A, they rounded a bend and came upon a group of a half dozen Indians traveling down the road toward Meadow Valley. The Indians were on horseback and leading heavily laden pack burros. As the wardens approached the mounted group, Mercer recognized one of them, an outlaw by the name of Jim Steel.

Jim Steel, or Indian Jim, as he was known, had ended up on the short end of an encounter with Mercer six months earlier when Mercer had caught him with an illegal deer. Mercer had taken the Indian before the Quincy judge, and the judge had imposed a light fine, giving the man a few weeks to pay. But Indian Jim had simply ignored the fine and disappeared into the forests. Now he was a wanted man with a warrant out for his arrest.

"Pull over," said Mercer urgently, and Johnston hit the brakes. As the car came to an abrupt stop, Mercer was out the door, and before Indian Jim could react, the warden had grabbed the bridle of his horse. The startled horse snorted and pulled back violently, and this action frightened several of the other animals. Soon there was pandemonium, with bucking horses and pack burros, and shouts and curses as the Indians tried to regain control. Mercer hung on for all he was worth.

During the confusion, one of the Indians, who had somehow acquired a baseball-sized rock, sidled his plunging mount to within striking distance of Mercer. Mercer, who didn't see him coming, was a second away from a crushed skull. But as the Indian raised his arm to deliver the blow, he was smashed in the face by a fist the size of a small ham. He toppled backward from his horse, unconscious, landing in the dirt with a thud. Mercer glanced over to see Johnston, standing over the inert body of the Indian, sucking on a bruised knuckle. The big man had arrived just in time.

An hour later, Indian Jim and another Indian with an angry purple welt below his left eye found themselves behind bars in the Plumas County jail.

The Flying Squad

Warden Gene Mercer, in his new home in Sacramento, stood peering into the mirror, pondering his first look at himself in uniform. He noted with satisfaction how the crisply pressed brown dress shirt bearing his badge was complemented nicely by the green 'peg top' pants, which were tucked neatly into the shined tops of his sixteen-inch lace-up boots. He adjusted the wide, basketweave Sam Brown belt so that his holstered Colt .38 rode squarely on his right hip, then he toyed with the strap that ran over his left shoulder, diagonally across his chest, supporting the gun side of his belt. Finally his attention was drawn to the new, stiff-brimmed, 'Smokey Bear' hat. He tried positioning it several ways, from dead straight to tilted rakishly over one eye, but finally decided on a rather conservative attitude with only a slight tilt to one side.

No doubt about it, Fish and Game had chosen a sharp-looking uniform for its wardens. But Mercer—as did most of the wardens—regarded the prospect of working in uniform with mixed emotions. True, uniforms would give the warden force a more professional appearance and perhaps an extra measure of public respect. But the wardens were long accustomed to wearing whatever clothes they chose, and old habits were hard to break.

The new uniforms represented only one of many changes that occurred in Mercer's life during the early months of 1937, for it was then that he took a transfer to Sacramento to become a member of a special new warden unit. Known as the Flying Squad, the new unit was intended by Fish and Game to be highly mobile, capable of responding immediately to special enforcement problems anywhere in the state. Wardens of the Flying Squad would be moved secretly into problem areas to work undercover on situations in which the local wardens were too well known to be effective. The squad was comprised of three two-man units—one based in Los Angeles, one in San Francisco, and one in Sacramento.

The chief of patrol at that time, Ed McCaulay, had contacted Mercer and asked him to consider a move to Sacramento to set up the Sacramento arm of the Flying Squad. Mercer had been on the promotion list for captain at the time, and McCaulay promised him a promotion to the soon-to-be-vacant captain's position in Los Baños when the job was completed.

It had been a tough decision for Mercer. He had loved his Quincy district, and his wife was happy there, but the chief had wanted him in Sacramento. And having always been a department man, this was no small consideration. Then, too, he couldn't ignore the advantages that captain's pay would provide for his family. The determining factor in his decision, however, was probably the lure of new challenges and adventures, but for whatever reasons, by March 17, the Mercers had moved to Sacramento.

*   *   *

In the early thirties, the department began hiring a new class of employees known as assistant wardens. These men, who came on at ninety dollars per month, did a variety of things for Fish and Game. Some went to hatcheries, some assisted in research projects, and were involved in depredation trapping, but most worked with the wardens in wildlife protection work. When the Flying Squad came into being, each of its three two-man units consisted of one regular warden and one of the new assistant wardens. Mercer's first Flying Squad partner was Assistant Warden Ed Hughes.

Mercer and Hughes first saw action together while awaiting a Flying Squad assignment in Sacramento. There had been reports of pheasant poaching in the farmland just west of Sacramento, an area known as the Yolo Bypass, and they were sent there to investigate. As it happened, it was Mercer's first day out in his new uniform.

After spending most of one day in the area of the reported problem, they finally heard shooting far to the south, along a levee that flanked a large canal running north and south. With their binoculars, they spotted two men carrying shotguns and apparently hunting in a northerly direction in the knee-deep grass along the levee. Mercer and Hughes crawled into some heavy cover farther north on the levee and watched as the suspects approached.

Any doubts the wardens may have had as to the guilt of the two approaching hunters were set to rest as the unsuspecting pair fired several more shots, killing at least one pheasant. Their hunt was then brought to an abrupt close when the two uniformed officers emerged from cover a few short yards ahead.

"State game wardens," shouted Mercer. "Stay where you are."

But after only a brief pause, the pheasant poachers wheeled in unison and took off at a dead run, abandoning several freshly killed pheasants as they fled. The wardens were close behind and the chase was on.

Ed Hughes had been an athlete and was renowned for his great speed afoot. He was in the lead as the chase began, but Mercer soon passed him "like a pay car passin' a bum" (Mercer's expression) and zeroed in on the more fleet-footed of the two fleeing poachers.

The chase led Mercer at full sprint along a path by the canal. When the panic-stricken poacher shot a wild glance over his shoulder and saw the hard-eyed warden bearing down on him, he took to the water in a last desperate effort to escape. He was thrashing wildly to gain the far bank as Mercer launched himself through the air and into the brown, silt-laden water—crisp new uniform, Smokey Bear hat, and all. He struck the chest-deep water with a great splash and lunged after his quarry. The poacher was frantically clambering up the opposite bank as Mercer caught up with him and grabbed him from behind by his belt. He hauled the struggling man back into the water and subdued him with a hammerlock.

"Hold it, ouch! I've had enough . . . I give up," gasped the badly winded poacher as Mercer bent his arm in a direction it wasn't intended to bend. The chase was over.

As Mercer dragged his man back across the canal, he noted with satisfaction that Hughes had done his part and captured the other poacher. After a short search in which he recovered a hastily abandoned shotgun and a couple of pheasants, Mercer started back to the patrol car, well satisfied with the afternoon's events.

As he led the thoroughly drenched and dejected poacher along, he paid little attention to the water squishing in his new sixteen-inch boots, or the mud and bits of pond weed clinging to his new uniform shirt, or the muddy water dripping from the sodden brim of his new Smokey Bear hat . . . for it had been a fine day.

Border Deer Poachers

It was the dead of winter when Warden Gene Mercer and Assistant Warden Gene Durney arrived in the Modoc County town of Alturas. While there was only patchy snow remaining from the last storm, it was bitter cold, with an icy wind blowing down from the Oregon border thirty-five miles to the north. Mercer parked the unmarked Chevrolet sedan on a side street in the main part of town, and the two wardens, dressed inconspicuously in civilian clothes, booked rooms in the hotel. After a quick meal in a small diner, they drove west out of town to get a look at the country in which they would be working for the next few nights.

It was Flying Squad business that brought them to Modoc County, where Oregon poachers were slipping into California and killing large numbers of mule deer. The problem seemed to be centered along Highway 139, between Alturas and the Oregon border, a long, lonely stretch of road that wound through the sage and juniper flats of the high desert country near the border. It was vast, largely uninhabited country—the favorite wintering area of the border mule deer.

Assistant Warden Gene Durney, assigned to assist Mercer in the operation, was a man whom Mercer had come to respect and trust—in fact they had become good friends. Durney was a man of medium height, medium build, and rather ordinary appearance, but beyond that there was nothing ordinary about him. Mercer knew him to be a highly intelligent, quick-witted, smooth-talking officer with a special gift for blending in with any group. These traits, combined with remarkably steady nerves, made him an excellent choice for undercover work. In years to come, as a regular warden, Durney would earn the reputation of being one of the most skillful and dedicated men in his profession.

Turning north at Canby, the wardens traveled another twenty miles into the very heart of the problem area. With some difficulty, they located a spot where they could get their car off the highway without leaving too obvious a trail in the remaining snow. It was their belief that the poaching was being done at night by spotlighters, and it was their plan to spend a few nights watching the highway to see what developed.

When they were tucked back away off the highway, they began to wonder if they were far enough from the road so as not to be illuminated by the headlights of passing cars. To find out, Durney went down the road about a hundred yards and climbed a juniper tree to wait for a car to pass. From that vantage point, he would be able to see if their vehicle could be spotted from the road. But there was no traffic on the highway, and the two men began what was to be a long, cold wait, with Durney perched in his juniper tree and Mercer huddled in the car. Hour after hour, the chilly night wore on, and not a single car appeared.

Durney was beginning to grow numb from the cold when the icy silence was suddenly shattered by Mercer's piercing call.

"Ugger dugger!"

Durney was startled at first, then he smiled in comprehension. This odd expression had sprung up between the two wardens as a sort of battle cry—a bit of nonsense that added a little humor to their lives.

After a chuckle, Durney returned the call.

"Ugger dugger!" he cried, his hands cupped around his mouth.

Then all was silent again as the two men settled down once more, hoping for something to break the monotony of the long winter night. It was not to be, however, and dawn found them cold, tired, and unsuccessful.

The following afternoon, after a few hours sleep at the hotel, they returned to the area to give it some close scrutiny during daylight. They passed the spot where they had spent the preceding night and continued up the road toward the border. Mile after mile, the landscape remained the same: rolling expanses of frozen sage and juniper stretching in all directions, with the snowbound Sierras rising off in the distance to the southwest.

Occasionally they saw deer—usually does with fawns, but now and then they spotted a large buck that had yet to shed its antlers. In some areas the deer were in small herds, standing alert with ears erect as they watched the car wind its way by. All were of the heavy-bodied, Rocky Mountain Mule Deer variety, fat and healthy, and prime bait for poachers.

The wardens continued on, and as they gradually gained altitude, they began to see pines scattered in with the junipers. Suddenly Durney told Mercer to stop the car. His keen eyes had spotted something out of place. Mercer brought the vehicle to an abrupt halt, then backed up a few yards. There in the sparse snow, a few feet off the road, was a small juniper branch that didn't belong there. Had it possibly been placed there as a marker? They soon verified this when they walked a short distance off the road and found blood and drag marks. A deer had been dragged to the road at this spot and loaded into a vehicle.

The fact that a marker had been used indicated that the poacher had not attempted to take the deer with him at the time of the kill. He had instead marked the spot so that the animal could be located later, either by himself or by a pickup man.

After dark that night, Mercer and Durney again positioned themselves to watch a lonely stretch of highway. Sometime after midnight, they heard an engine and then a slow-moving car crept by, its headlights sweeping a narrow path through the darkness. The driver was maneuvering the vehicle as though he was looking for something.

The wardens were almost certain that the vehicle, which had come from the direction of the Oregon border, contained a poacher or at least a pickup man for a poacher. But since they were reasonably sure that any poacher-killed deer would be taken back to Oregon, they chose to let the vehicle go on its way. They would commit themselves only if the vehicle returned that night.

As it happened, the vehicle did return. Now it was headed toward Oregon, and it was traveling at a normal rate of speed. This presented the wardens with something of a dilemma: they had heard no shooting nor had they seen anyone working a spotlight, yet the behavior of the driver of the vehicle was highly suspicious. If they tipped their hand and made a stop of the vehicle, they risked blowing their whole operation. On the other hand, the vehicle could be the one they were looking for and could contain a deer or two. They figured their chances to be about fifty-fifty, and, after considerable deliberation, they decided to make the stop.

The vehicle responded immediately to Mercer's red-handkerchief-covered light and pulled to a stop. The two wardens moved quickly up either side of the vehicle, anxious to see the worried face and nervous hands that would be the first indicators of success. Instead, they found a totally calm young woman at the wheel.

"State game wardens," said Mercer, displaying his badge.

"What's the trouble, officer?" the young woman asked, a look of mock concern on her face.

"Sorry to bother you, ma'am, but we've had some poaching problems around here lately. Would you mind if we have a quick look in your trunk?"

"Not at all," she said, "It's open, help yourself."

Durney walked around and popped open the trunk lid, then looked back at Mercer and shook his head.

"Ma'am, could I ask what you're doing out here tonight?" Mercer asked.

"Just out for a ride," she said, smiling smugly.

Mercer clenched his teeth as it dawned on him—the woman was a decoy. She had done her job well, luring the game wardens from hiding and sparing her husband or boyfriend a bad brush with the law.

"You're free to go, ma'am," said Mercer, the friendly tone now absent from his voice.

Mercer and Durney watched her drive away, disgusted with themselves for falling for the trick. But with the information at hand, their decision had been logical. Now it was time to stop and reassess the situation. They had to admit that they were gaining new respect for their adversaries.

The stop of the woman had been an unfortunate thing, but Mercer felt that he and Durney still had a chance. He believed there to be more than one clan of poachers operating in the area, and there was a good chance other poachers wouldn't hear about the stop. So the two wardens decided to work the area a few more nights.

It should be remembered that Mercer and Durney were working completely undercover; they wore plain clothes and drove an unmarked car. Therefore, two nights later, when they met and passed a slow-moving vehicle and were scrutinized by three sets of wary eyes, they caused no particular alarm. The wardens continued on their way until they were well out of sight of the suspected violators, then turned around.

Driving now by starlight and the dim glow of a sliver of a moon, they slowly overtook the suspect vehicle. When it came into view, they knew their luck had changed. A bright spotlight was being worked from the vehicle and it cast great arcs of light across the frozen juniper flats, first from one side of the vehicle and then from the other.

The wardens carefully approached to within fifty yards of the vehicle, then maintained that station as the unsuspecting violators crept along, scanning the countryside for game. It was only a short time before brake lights flashed on and the spotlight came to rest on two bright reflective eyes off to the left, where a doe stood transfixed in the brilliant beam. A rifle barrel was leveled out the window and it bucked sharply as the shot rang out. The stricken doe went briefly to her knees, then was up and bounding through a snowdrift. Doors flew open and two men with rifles leapt from the vehicle in pursuit.

Mercer and Durney, invisible in the darkness to the rear, waited like foxes poised to pounce on a covey of quail.

"We'll take 'em when they get back to the car," said Mercer, squinting into the darkness.

But, unfortunately, their luck took a turn for the worse when headlights appeared up ahead, coming toward them. Mercer couldn't believe it—on a stretch of highway that often went a full night without traffic, a car was coming at the worst possible time. As it approached, it illuminated the whole scene, including the two disgusted wardens in the patrol car. Mercer had to show his lights to avoid being struck by the oncoming vehicle. It was a rotten piece of luck.

The poachers understood their peril immediately. The two on foot made no attempt to get back to their car, but hightailed it away into the darkness. The driver wasn't so lucky. The wardens were quickly upon him before he could make any attempt to escape. Durney then set out in pursuit of the two on foot.

It wasn't too difficult for Durney to follow their trail at first, for it was impossible for them to avoid all the patches of snow. He jogged along easily in the moonlight, conserving his strength, eyes straining to pick up the tracks. After about a quarter mile, he encountered a rifle abandoned in the snow.

"At least I got a piece of 'em," he thought, as he reached down and picked up the weapon. But he was never able to catch up with the two men that night. They had doubled back to the road after a mile or so and had traveled on the snow-free pavement for a while. In the darkness, Durney was unable to determine where they left the road again. He had no choice but to return to the vehicles with only the abandoned rifle to show for his efforts.

A search of the poacher's vehicle revealed evidence that suggested they had killed many deer from it over a period of time. There was dried blood and deer hair and—to the amazement of the wardens—literally hundreds of spent rifle cartridges on the floor.

The wardens recovered the doe and took their one prisoner to Alturas, where he was booked into jail. The wardens were bitter over the escape of the other two poachers, but at least they had the satisfaction of knowing that the two men had undoubtedly spent a miserable night out in the snow.

Although Mercer and Durney were far from satisfied with the way things worked out, it was still an important case. The driver was sentenced to thirty days in jail, lost his rifle, and was fined five hundred dollars, an incredible sum at the time. More important, however, the word spread, and the incident proved to be a great deterrent against further poaching in that part of the state for a good while.

Alturas Abs

Warden Gene Mercer and Assistant Warden Gene Durney waited expectantly at their table as the waitress arrived with the main course of their dinner.

"You're gonna like this," she said with a smile, as she set the steaming platters before them.

Mercer regarded the chef's handiwork with genuine appreciation. The thin, light-colored slices of fine-grained meat lay neatly arranged, tastefully garnished and drenched in a mild garlic-butter sauce. Opposite the meat was a large baked potato and a colorful mixed vegetable dish. Not only was the arrangement pleasing to the eye, but there emanated from it a tantalizing seafood aroma.

At the first bite, Mercer looked over at Durney and nodded his head in affirmation. There was no mistaking the delicate taste and mildly rubbery consistency.

"No doubt about it," said Mercer. "It's definitely abalone."

"No doubt about it," agreed Durney.

It had been only a few weeks since the border deer poacher assignment, and already Mercer and Durney were back in Alturas again. This time they were to work on another deer poaching problem that was occurring somewhere between Alturas and Lakeview. They had slipped quietly into town earlier that afternoon, again undercover, and they had drawn little attention when they booked rooms in the Niles Hotel.

At dinner that night at the hotel restaurant, they were surprised to see abalone on the menu. Since it happened to be the closed season for abalone, and abalone could not be sold or even possessed legally, they were immediately interested. When the waitress arrived to take their orders, both men had ordered abalone.

After their meal, and after they each had saved a small portion of the tasty shellfish for evidence purposes, they located the restaurant owner, introduced themselves, and took him aside. The restaurant owner, a small, swarthy man named Anthony Bova, squirmed uncomfortably as the wardens displayed their badges. Mercer conducted the interrogation of Bova with great care, his main objective being to come away with enough information to trace the illegal abalone back to its source.

"Mr. Bova, you're in some trouble," Mercer began. "Selling abalone this time of year is a serious offense. But we're going to level with you: we want the people who supplied you with the abalone. We're a lot more interested in catching *them* than giving *you* a hard time. You've got the option of cooperating with us— and if you do, it'll go a lot easier for you."

"What do you want me to do?" asked Bova.

"First of all, we want you to tell us who your supplier is," said Mercer.

Bova looked down at the floor, obviously thinking, then returned his gaze to Mercer.

"If I tell you, are you gonna let me go?" he asked.

"We can't let you off entirely," said Mercer, "but we won't take you to jail, and we won't close down your place—and we'll make sure the right people know you helped us."

Bova considered this information for a few seconds, then made his decision.

"I'll tell you whatever you wanna know," he said. "I get the abalone from Pacific Seafood. They come through here twice a week. They should be here again day after tomorrow."

"All right," said Mercer. "Now, we don't want you to mention this to anyone. Just go on about your business as usual."

Following some additional instructions to Bova, the wardens left the restaurant.

Two days later, an old, unmarked military ambulance pulled up to the rear service entrance of the Niles Hotel. Pacific Seafood had arrived. The driver stepped to the rear, threw open the double doors, and began sorting through various wooden crates packed in crushed ice. When he turned around, he was face-to-face with the law.

Mercer again did the interrogation, and the driver—who turned out to be the owner and sole employee of Pacific Seafood—promptly told the whole story. He was essentially a middleman, purchasing fish from either of two seafood companies in Sacramento and reselling it to restaurants and markets in various towns in the northeastern corner of the state. He readily admitted to having purchased the abalone from the New Canton Fish Company in Sacramento.

While Durney searched the makeshift fish truck and located about fifteen pounds of fresh abalone, Mercer had the telephone operator put a call through to Walnut Grove. A few minutes later he was talking, via a rather shaky connection, to Warden Charlie Sibeck.

Charlie Sibeck was well acquainted with the New Canton Fish Company. The company had long been suspected of illegal trade in fish products, and less than an hour after Mercer's call, Sibeck and two other wardens raided the place. They found more than forty pounds of illegal abalone.

Despite the owner's complaints, voiced loudly in a rapid-fire mixture of pidgin English and Chinese, the wardens seized all his abalone, and various other items of salty contraband, and took him immediately before a Sacramento judge. But all efforts by Sibeck to induce the owner to divulge the identity of the diver—the man who had actually harvested the abalone—proved fruitless.

The Sacramento judge accepted a guilty plea from the Chinese fish merchant, sentenced him to a heavy fine, then announced his decision to dispose of the forty pounds of confiscated abalone steaks himself.

Back in Alturas, Mercer and Durney resumed their original assignment.

Jerky Camp

A rifle shot boomed in the distance, and Jake McGrath awoke with a start. Another shot followed, its echo rolling through the winter night like distant thunder. McGrath rolled out of bed and peered through a window into the darkness. It was after midnight, the second night in a row that he had been awakened by shooting. From his snug cabin on a timbered ridge overlooking the snowbound Genesee Valley, he judged the shots to have come from somewhere a mile or so to the east. But he could see nothing ... nothing but the dark outline of the Sierras against a moonless sky.

"Damned poachers," he muttered, as he climbed back into bed, mulling the situation over in his mind.

Others had heard the shooting too. The talk in nearby Taylorsville was that it had begun a few weeks earlier— about the time some strangers had set up a camp in a secluded spot near the mouth of Henchman Creek.

"Must be shootin' 'em to sell," McGrath thought, "and that's goin' too far." In the morning he would call Mercer.

*   *   *

Warden Gene Mercer was almost out the door when the phone rang. He turned and headed back. He had appointments to keep and was running late, but he was too good a warden to miss a call. He picked up the phone.

"Hello, Mercer? This is McGrath. We've got a problem up here." Mercer listened intently as McGrath filled him in on the details.

It was January of 1938. Ten months had passed since Mercer had reluctantly left his mountain patrol district in Plumas County to join Fish and Game's newly formed Flying Squad in Sacramento. The Chief of Patrol, aware of Mercer's abilities, had requested him for the job, and Mercer had felt compelled to accept.

As one of the Flying Squad's traveling troubleshooters, Mercer was sent wherever needed to work undercover, assisting the resident wardens with particularly troublesome poaching problems. Occasionally he passed through his beloved Plumas County, but by then it belonged to another warden. So when McGrath called, the poaching problem in the Genesee Valley should not have been Mercer's concern. But there were some of his old informants, like McGrath, who had learned to trust him over the years and would deal with no one else.

Mercer thanked McGrath for the tip, then immediately called Warden Ed Johnson in Quincy. Johnson, a young, hard-working warden, was doing his best to replace Mercer in Plumas County. Upon receiving McGrath's information, Johnson asked Mercer for help. Facing a possible commercial poaching operation, Johnson felt that Mercer's assistance would be invaluable. But it came at a bad time for Mercer, who explained that he could easily come the following day, but that it would be difficult for him to get away before then. Johnson asked him to try.

"Damn," said Mercer, as he hung up the receiver. "Why couldn't this have come tomorrow?"

He hated these decisions. He was stuck with commitments that day—important commitments that would be difficult to put off. Yet McGrath's information had a ring of urgency about it, and something in Mercer—an instinct he had developed over the years— was telling him to drop everything and go.

Turning to the phone again, he made some hurried calls and apologies, and within the hour he was headed for Plumas County. With him was his good friend Assistant Warden Gene Durney, who like Mercer would someday be regarded as one of the best of California's Fish and Game wardens.

Mercer and Durney pulled into Quincy shortly before noon. After a brief discussion with Johnson, it was decided that the three of them would simply pay a surprise visit to the camp on Henchman Creek and see what they could find. Less than an hour later, they had completed the thirty-five-mile drive to the area and were sneaking along, on foot, through eight inches of new snow.

When they reached the spot where the icy waters of Henchman Creek spilled into Indian Creek, they paused. They could see tracks in the snow where vehicles had left the main road to follow the east bank of Henchman Creek into a wooded canyon. A quarter mile up the canyon, thin plumes of smoke rose lazily through the pines.

The wardens spread out as they crept on through the snow toward the source of the smoke. Mercer immediately began to notice unusual numbers of coyote and fox tracks that were apparently leading to and from the direction of the camp. At one point, he spotted a fresh hind leg bone of a deer lying in the snow, and it struck him as strange that some predator had abandoned it there. As he continued on, his pulse quickened, the way it always did when action was imminent. He knew, for no reason he could explain, that they were on to something good.

Soon they could make out the camp through the trees. It was situated in a small meadow a few yards from the creek. There were two rectangular wall tents and a much larger, circular pole tent, a column of smoke rising from each. A light military flatbed truck and a sedan were parked nearby.

Suddenly Durney motioned urgently for Mercer to come. He was staring down at something in a shallow ravine about fifty yards below the camp. Mercer hurried over and was astonished to see a great pile of fresh deer bones half buried in the snow. A distinct trail led from the pile of bones to the camp.

Mercer kicked through the pile, counting and figuring, and determined that he was looking at the bones of at least thirty deer. Just then a bit of a breeze brought a wisp of woodsmoke to his nostrils, bearing with it the savory, smokehouse aroma of curing meat.

The wardens spread out again to approach the camp from different directions. Soon they could hear voices and occasional laughter, apparently coming from the pole tent. Mercer cautiously approached one of the wall tents and peeked through the flap. The interior was dark with smoke, but he could make out what appeared to be large racks of meat drying above a low fire. The second wall tent contained more of the same.

The wardens then silently closed in on the pole tent, careful to avoid casting shadows on the gray canvas. It was plain from the loud conversation within that the wardens had not yet been detected. Mercer signaled Durney to stand back and cover them while he and Johnson made their move.

Inside the round tent, three grimy, unshaven individuals sat on stools at a small table, well into the task of cutting up the two deer they had killed the night before. One of the men worked swiftly with a thin-bladed boning knife, slicing large chunks of meat from a hind quarter of a large doe. The other two men were cutting the chunks into strips and tossing them into a galvanized tub of brine. Near one side of the table were several additional venison quarters laid out on a tarp, while on the opposite side, there was a growing pile of bones. The men talked and laughed as they worked.

They were discussing plans for wild times in the city

with the cash they would get from the sale of their jerky. They had dried around two thousand pounds of deer meat during their three-week stay in the mountains, and the resulting 250 pounds of jerky would be worth a tidy sum. In the bars and taverns of San Francisco—where they spent most of their time—venison jerky would sell for about six dollars a pound.

They had decided to finish up with the deer they had killed the night before, then pack up and head back to the city. All three were in agreement that they had pressed their luck far enough.

As they continued their lively conversation, they failed to hear the soft crunch of approaching footsteps in the snow outside the tent. They were therefore totally surprised when suddenly the tent flap was thrown open and they found themselves face-to-face with the law.

"State game wardens, nobody move!" shouted Mercer. One of the poachers started to reach for a rifle on his cot, but then thought better of it as he felt Mercer's eyes boring holes in him. The wardens were armed and ready, with the look of men it would not be wise to cross.

"Leave your knives on the table and come on out," instructed Mercer. The three men grudgingly complied. They stood sullenly, half in shock, as the wardens handcuffed them to their flatbed truck.

With the prisoners secured, the wardens began a systematic search of the camp. Inside the wall tents—which were in fact portable smokehouses—the wardens found old metal bedsprings being used as racks on which strips of deer meat were suspended over smoldering alder-wood fires. Mercer sampled a piece of the jerky and found it to be delicious, the best he had ever tasted.

Inside the cab of the flatbed truck, the wardens found over a dozen string-tied flour sacks, each containing about twenty pounds of jerky. They loaded these into their suspects' sedan—which they had decided to commandeer—along with more than 120 pounds of fresh deer meat that they found in the pole tent. They also seized a variety of guns, ammunition, and knives, plus a pair of spotlights.

After finishing their search, the wardens loaded up their prisoners and the remainder of the evidence, and set out for Greenville. They were delighted with their good fortune, for with them in the patrol car and the commandeered sedan were all the essential elements of the most awesome deer case they had ever heard of.

Mercer, however, took a moment to reflect on the fact that the poachers had nearly won. They had been ready to pull out. Had Mercer waited the extra day to act, the jerky camp would have been gone, and only the tramped-down snow and the huge pile of deer bones would have remained to tell the grim tale. But it was the wardens' turn to be lucky. By dark that night the poachers were behind bars in Greenville and the wardens were winding their way through the snow-covered forest toward Quincy. They were in high spirits as they drove along, recounting the day's events, each aglow with the special satisfaction that good wardens experience when they catch somebody who really deserves catching.

Tahoe
Setliners

Warden Gene Mercer gazed out across the vast expanse of cobalt blue water and was once again deeply moved by its awesome beauty. High in the rugged Sierras, it lay shimmering in the winter sunlight, twenty miles long and fourteen wide, its rocky shores cloaked in a blanket of new snow. Of all the earthly wonders he had encountered so far in his life, Mercer regarded Lake Tahoe as something special. Standing beside him, Assistant Warden Gene Durney shared similar thoughts.

Returning his mind to the business at hand, Mercer rested his elbows on the hood of the new Chevrolet undercover vehicle and focused his binoculars on a series of wooden piers jutting out from the northwest shore of the lake. Landward from each pier, on the snowy hillsides, there were lodges and cottages—the resorts and summer homes of the wealthy. Most appeared deserted, but there was smoke rising from the chimneys of a few. Mercer knew that only the hired caretakers would be present this time of the year, and it was illegal activity on the part of these caretakers that he and Durney had come to investigate.

The problem was setlining. The local warden was

certain that the caretakers of the summer homes were operating long, multi-hook setlines from the boat piers and were catching large numbers of lake trout. But when he tried to investigate, the caretakers were always warned by means of the new telephone system that had recently been installed. He had tried everything, including an approach at night by rowboat, but the results were always the same: someone would see him leave town, note his direction of travel, and the setliners would be warned by telephone. It was a frustrating problem, one he finally decided to turn over to the Flying Squad.

Upon receiving orders to proceed to Lake Tahoe, Mercer had again asked specifically for Gene Durney to assist him with the assignment. Mercer enjoyed working with Durney, and the two of them made a formidable team. They had chosen Truckee as their base of operations and upon their arrival, they had booked rooms at the Riverside Hotel. After a quick lunch, they had driven to the lake to get a feel for the country.

Taking the recently snowplowed road that followed the western shore, they had headed south until the two-mile stretch of resort shoreline came into view. There they had pulled off at a wide spot for a look.

"I hope you brought your long johns," said Mercer, as he squinted through the binoculars. "This is gonna be chilly business."

The following morning, shortly after dawn, the wardens found a spot to leave the car, then plowed their way on foot through thigh-deep snow to a low ridge a few hundred yards from the first resort. After hollowing out a nest in a snowdrift and lining it with a small tarp, they settled down to watch. Within the first hour, they had their first bit of good luck.

A man carrying a burlap sack emerged from the caretaker's quarters and followed a trail down through the snow to the boat dock. He walked to the end of the dock, then paused to look around. Satisfied that he was alone, he knelt down and began pulling in a line that was tied off on the end of the dock. Hand over hand, he brought it in, carefully arranging it on the dock to prevent its tangling. At intervals on the line there were cedar floats attached, and baited hooks on short dropper lines were suspended beneath each float.

As the wardens watched, the suspect pulled in a fish on one of the droppers, a bronze-backed Mackinaw trout of about five pounds. It struggled weakly as the man hoisted it onto the dock, its strength long since depleted from hours of fighting the setline. The suspect struck the fish a sharp blow to the head with a short section of broom handle, then unhooked it and slipped it into the burlap sack.

The man removed two more large trout from the line before he reached the end and pulled the sash weight anchor up onto the dock. He then baited the empty hooks with dead minnows and carefully arranged the wooden floats along one edge of the dock. When all was in order, he tied one end of a long cord to the sash weight anchor, which was still lying on the dock, and walked up the dock back to the bank, carefully feeding out the cord as he went. He followed the shoreline a hundred feet, then walked out onto the next boat dock, still feeding out cord. At the end of this dock he turned and started pulling in the cord as fast as he could. From the first dock, the sash weight anchor splashed into the water, followed one after the other by the dozen or so cedar floats. It went smoothly, obviously a well-practiced maneuver, and in a few seconds the suspect had the dripping sash weight in his hands and the setline was stretched taut between the two docks. He untied the cord and, when satisfied that the setline was straight and without tangles, he tossed in the sash weight anchor and watched it sink through the crystal-clear water, fifteen feet to the bottom. Now all that was visible on the surface was the series of wooden floats bobbing on the wind-rippled surface. The suspect then picked up the bag of fish, glanced quickly around, and started back to his cabin.

Mercer looked over at Durney, who had been busily scribbling notes on a lined pad. Mercer, using his binoculars, had made careful observations concerning the setliner's physical appearance, and Durney had taken this and other information down on paper.

"There's number one," said Mercer, as he and Durney gathered up the tarp and started back through the deep snow to their car.

The following day, they watched another suspect work a pair of similar setlines from the pier at the next resort, a quarter mile down the shoreline from the first. Things were shaping up.

Day after day, they continued their chilly stakeouts, and by the end of one week they had made good observations on a total of six suspects.

"I think that's all of 'em," said Mercer, as they drove back to Truckee one evening. "We'll hit 'em in the morning."

The sun was barely on the water as the wardens reached the lake the following morning, but Mercer seemed in no hurry to get to the first resort. Durney could see that something was bothering him.

"You know," said Mercer, "when we pinch the first one, he'll telephone the others and we'll be out of luck."

He was right. It was a real problem. They needed hard evidence to go with their observations of the past few days. They needed the setlines and some illegally taken fish to assure conviction of the suspects. But it was highly unlikely that the wardens would get anything if the suspects were warned.

Mercer mulled the problem over and over in his mind as he drove along, then suddenly it came to him. Smiling to himself, he pulled the Chevrolet to a sudden stop and hopped out. Durney watched curiously as Mercer went around to the back, dug around in the tool kit, and came up with a pair of heavy side-cutters. He then turned, stuffed the tool in his hip pocket, and gazed up at the telephone pole a few feet away.

"You're not thinkin' what I think you're thinkin'," said Durney.

Without bothering to reply, Mercer approached the pole, wrapped his arms around it, and started shinnying his way up. Upon reaching the top, he locked his legs around the pole and applied his side-cutters to the copper telephone wire. The wire parted with a loud metallic twang, and Mercer looked down at Durney with a grin.

"That ought to slow 'em down," he said.

Five minutes later, they pulled into the driveway of the first resort. The caretaker, suspect number one, met them at the door.

"Good morning, sir," said Mercer, displaying his badge. "We're state game wardens and we're here to talk to you about your setline."

"Setline?" said the caretaker, "What setline?"

"Well, let's take a walk down to the dock and we'll show you," said Mercer.

The caretaker saw no choice but to follow the wardens as they headed for the dock.

When the three men reached the boat dock, the caretaker's wife, who had witnessed the entire exchange, hurried to the wall-mounted telephone. She lifted the receiver, and cranked furiously on the bell handle. Putting the receiver to her ear, she listened anxiously, but there was nothing. She cranked the handle again. Still nothing. There would be no warning to her friends down the way.

The wardens worked swiftly, gathering in the setline— to which was attached a pair of large Mackinaw trout— and issuing a citation to the unhappy suspect. They then hurried on their way to the next resort complex.

At the second place, they again achieved complete surprise, and Mercer wrote the citation while Durney pulled in the two setlines.

And so it went. They made a clean sweep that day, gathering a total of nine setlines, a dozen and a half beautiful lake trout, and six disgruntled violators. It would be a nice, neat package to present to the local judge. "Not a bad piece of work," said Mercer, as he and Durney stowed their evidence in the new Chevy and started back for Truckee. They hadn't gone far when they passed a telephone company truck parked beside the roadway. They grinned at each other, then Mercer honked and waved at the lineman, perched high on a pole, making some emergency repairs.

Delta
Ambush

Evening had come to the Delta. A red glow to the west was all that remained of the summer sun, which a quarter hour earlier had disappeared somewhere beyond the Golden Gate. Warden Charlie Sibeck eased back on the throttle of the old Rainbow II patrol boat, allowing the bow to wedge a path through the band of shoreline tules and slide gently to a stop against a mud bank. He cut the engine and walked forward as Warden Gene Mercer secured the bow line to a willow snag. From the raised forward deck, the wardens could look out over the tules and view several miles of Delta marsh.

The area known as the Delta is a vast and bewildering maze of tule marshes, willow-covered islands, and twisting waterways. Forty miles across in places, most of it accessible only by boat, it is similar in many respects to the great marshlands of the East Coast. Situated in California's midsection, the Delta marks the confluence of the Sacramento and San Joaquin Rivers, and the other streams that drain California's great central valley. It is an area of transition, where fresh and salt waters meet, an area heavily affected by tidal surges of the Pacific Ocean. Crammed full of fish and wildlife, as it was in the thirties, it was the natural haunt of all types of game violators—and men like Charlie Sibeck were assigned there to deal with them.

Not all wardens were suited for Delta patrol, for it was an awesome, intimidating place to work in those days. Not only was it confusing geographically—an easy place to get lost—but there were clouds of biting mosquitoes to contend with, not to mention the bone-chilling tule fog that could materialize in seconds and leave a man blind and helpless miles from anywhere. And most threatening, there were the Delta outlaws, among the most ruthless and dangerous anywhere. More than one warden had met his death in some remote reach of the Delta in lethal confrontations with violators. No, the Delta was no place for any but the toughest and most fearless of wardens.

Charlie Sibeck definitely fell into this category, and he soon found that Gene Mercer, who was assigned to work with him in between Flying Squad assignments, was more than equal to the challenges as well.

It was mostly night work in places like Casche Slough, Chain Island, and Big Break, and the price of a good case was many long, frustrating hours of surveillance work. But Mercer loved chasing poachers wherever he could find them and found the Delta an interesting change.

It was Sibeck's never-ending pursuit of outlaw gill-netters that brought him and Mercer to Grizzly Bay that night. It would be their third all-night patrol there in as many nights, working on an informant's tip that had yet to pay off. But catching gill-netters was never easy.

As a group, the gill-netters were a cunning, intelligent bunch. Most were from well-known families that had produced outlaw fishermen for generations. Many, in fact, were the sons and grandsons of the same outlaws that Jack London wrote about in his book *Tales of the Fish Patrol* at the turn of the century. They would set out their long gill nets only in the dark of night, and to pursue these men through the hidden channels and waterways they had known since childhood was like chasing shadows.

As darkness gathered, the wardens peered around for one last look in the dwindling light. To the south, beyond the low range of barren foothills, Mount Diablo loomed black against the evening sky. To the north, Grizzly Bay lay spread out before them, dark and brooding, a somehow unfriendly expanse of murky water. It was low tide, and the exposed mud flats tainted the cool night air with a heavy, seashore smell.

On the flood tide, the main upstream currents swelled into Grizzly Bay—a blind pocket four miles across—and flowed around its perimeter to exit not far from the entrance. Due to its configuration and odd current patterns, the bay was a natural trap to the great schools of migrating king salmon and striped bass. Caught in Grizzly Bay, they would mill around in temporary confusion, searching for the way out to resume their spawning journeys. But while in the bay, these valuable fish were highly vulnerable—easy and tempting prey for the gill-netters of the waterfront Delta towns.

"The tide's comin' in now," said Sibeck. "If they show up tonight, it'll probably be around midnight." The wardens settled down to wait, drinking coffee, telling stories, and swatting mosquitoes.

*   *   *

Five miles to the south, from a ramshackle dock near the Pittsburg waterfront, Anthony Demetras made a quiet departure. Upon reaching the main channel, he spun the wheel of his eighteen-foot net boat, swinging the bow until it lined up with the north star. Up forward, reclining comfortably in a huge mound of piled gill-net, Frank Coito puffed on a cigarette and stared up at the sky. The main branch of the river here was more than a half mile wide, and it was several minutes before the dark outline of the north bank came into view.

Demetras made no attempt to change course or speed, continuing directly toward the willow-choked shoreline. When it appeared he would soon run aground, an opening suddenly appeared, and he swung into the narrow channel known as Spoonbill Cut. The low, rhythmic thumping of the diesel engine was more apparent now in the narrow confines of Spoonbill, but after a mile or so, they broke out into Honker Bay and things seemed quieter again. They passed the decaying remains of a long-wrecked river barge, its broken skeleton lying tilted against the bank, half exposed by the low tide. They cleared Honker Bay and after threading their way through a confusing series of small islands, they rounded a point and idled quietly into Grizzly Bay.

Upon entering the famous fishing grounds, Demetras hugged the south shore, holding the engine at minimum speed. Gill-netting had become risky business, and it paid to follow certain precautions. He continued for only a short distance before he cut the engine to look and listen. Grizzly Bay lay becalmed before them, silver in the moonlight, and all was quiet.

In the old days, Demetras would have continued straight across the bay to his grandfather's cabin perched on pilings amid a cluster of other remote cabins in the narrow inlet known as Rat Catcher Cut. But things were different now.

Rat Catcher Cut was the only habitation anywhere on Grizzly Bay, the shores of which were otherwise surrounded by miles of tule flats. The cut was on the southeast side of the bay, directly opposite the best fishing grounds. But the wardens had become aware of the illegal activities there and had begun watching it closely. Several well-known netters, including some of the best of the old timers, had been pounced upon by wardens there and had ended up losing their boats and nets.

No, the good fishing off Rat Catcher was no longer worth the risk. Demetras had given it up, reasoning that by staying near the entrance to the bay, a good mile and a half west of Rat Catcher Cut, he would be less apt to encounter wardens—and if they did appear, he would have a better chance of escaping to any of a dozen hidden channels outside the bay.

Satisfied that there were at least no immediate dangers, Demetras fired the engine and steered directly away from the shore. A hundred yards out, where instinct told him it was right, he throttled back and made a sharp turn back toward shore. With the bow now pointed shoreward, he shifted to reverse and backed down slowly. Coito was ready up forward and dropped a cement net-anchor over the side, and then, as Demetras continued backing down, he played out the net. Hand over hand, he fed the bundle of cotton mesh over the bow, the lead weights making a soft thumping sound as they bumped across the battered gunwale, scarred and furrowed from years of such use. It took only three or four minutes to feed out the entire net, and upon reaching the end, Coito anchored it with another twenty-five-pound concrete weight.

Cork floats attached every few feet supported the top of the net at the water's surface, while lead weights at intervals along the bottom assured that it would hang vertically in the water. From float line to lead line, it was only twelve feet deep, but it was more than an eighth of a mile long. Stretched taut and anchored at each end, it hung like the net of some huge underwater tennis court. It was entirely handmade and had cost Demetras more than six thousand dollars.

Finished with his immediate task, Coito stood up and followed the float line with his eye. The cork floats, barely visible in the moonlight, stretched off into the distance like dark beads on a string. As he watched, one of the floats a few yards out was jerked violently on the surface. Ten feet below, a thirty-pound king salmon had struck the net and become entangled. At first contact with the net, the big fish had bulled its way partially through the seven-inch mesh, but then, unable to force its way through, it had thrashed wildly, the cotton cords fouling in its gills. Now, securely trapped, it would slowly drown.

Coito nodded with satisfaction as Demetras headed the boat back to shore. Now they would hold tight in the tules until it was time to pull the net.

*   *   *

Less than a quarter mile east along the shoreline, wardens Sibeck and Mercer watched silently from the hidden deck of the Rainbow II. Sibeck peered through his binoculars, his eyes burning with a predatory gleam.

"Looks like they got the net out," he whispered. "Now we wait."

Neither warden had heard the net boat approach. It had just suddenly appeared, a dark silhouette in the moonlight. While visibility was limited, and Mercer couldn't tell what was going on in the boat, Sibeck knew exactly what was happening. He had seen it many times before. So now they waited for the violators to make their next move.

Three hours later, with the tide just beginning to ebb, the net boat again appeared.

"There they are," whispered Sibeck. "They're pullin' the net. Now, we give 'em a little more rope to hang themselves." Sibeck had learned over the years that netters were most vulnerable when in the middle of pulling their nets. When caught with the net half in and half out of the boat, they couldn't run for it without first cutting the net or throwing overboard what net they had in the boat. Either way, it took time—time enough to give the wardens an edge. And if the netters had a bunch of net-marked fish on board, so much the better.

After a few tense minutes of simply waiting, Sibeck signaled Mercer to untie the bow line. Then, using an oar, he silently poled the Rainbow II back through the tules into open water. With the tide on the ebb, the current caught the Rainbow and slowly carried it westward toward the net boat. Sibeck then moved quietly to the controls, ready to start the engine and charge forward. Mercer, tense with excitement, used the oar to keep the Rainbow's bow pointed directly at the net boat so as to present the narrowest silhouette.

*   *   *

Despite the early morning chill, Frank Coito sweated freely as he labored at pulling the heavy, fish-laden net. It wasn't just hard work that brought on the perspiration, but apprehension as well, for Coito knew full well that this was the most hazardous part of the operation. If there were wardens out there, they'd be coming soon. Demetras was equally nervous as he removed the numerous salmon from the net and tossed them aft onto the deck, which was already completely covered with fish. They worked swiftly, but stopped often to listen and peer out across the black waters for signs of wardens.

It was Coito who saw it first, a dark object outlined against the barely visible shoreline two hundred yards to the south.

"Tony," he whispered, pointing towards it.

Demetras turned and followed the shoreline with his eyes. Upon spotting the object, he grabbed a pair of battered binoculars from the deckhouse and peered through them.

"I think it's a boat," he said, still squinting through the binoculars. "I don't like this at all." Suddenly he dropped the binoculars and hurried toward the bow.

"Dump the net," he said urgently, as he grabbed a big armload of net and struggled toward the gunwale with it. Coito jumped to assist him and they worked frantically to get the great pile of sodden net over the side.

On the Rainbow II, Charlie Sibeck had watched all this through his own pair of binoculars. "They've seen us," he said, as he reached for the controls.

At a touch of the starter, the big gas engine roared to life and the Rainbow II shot forward. Mercer, near the bow, was nearly toppled over. Sibeck steered straight for the net boat, the patrol boat's throttle wide open.

Aboard the net boat, the two outlaws, working feverishly, pushed the last of the net overboard and Demetras jumped to the controls. The old diesel coughed to a start, emitting a cloud of smoke, and Demetras threw it into gear. As it plowed ahead, he instinctively steered away from the fast-approaching patrol boat. Coito frantically began throwing the salmon overboard, each fish bearing the telltale, incriminating marks of the gill net.

Demetras, after glancing back and realizing that he had no chance of outrunning the patrol boat, changed course and headed for the nearest point of land. If he could make it to shore and beach the boat, he and Coito could escape on foot and lose themselves in the dense tules. It was their only chance.

In the patrol boat, Sibeck guessed immediately what the outlaws had in mind, and he altered course to cut them off. The Rainbow II closed rapidly on the fleeing net boat, and soon the wardens could make out the figures of both outlaws, one of whom was chucking fish over the side. Sibeck maintained the collision course, and Mercer crouched low on the forward deck, ready for action.

The Rainbow roared up on the net boat, and Sibeck swung to a parallel course only a few feet away.

"State game wardens," he yelled. "Cut your engine."

But when the driver made no move to stop, Sibeck veered toward it, and the two boats came together with a sharp jolt. Mercer was ready and sprang from the Rainbow's bow, landing in the net boat in a pile of dead salmon. Recovering quickly, he scrambled over and grabbed Demetras from behind.

"Shut 'er down," he yelled, over the loud clatter of the engines.

Demetras, upon feeling the powerful fingers gripping

the back of his neck, throttled back and brought the net boat to a stop.

But Coito wasn't ready to give up. Crouched low up forward, he glanced over at the bank, a mere fifty yards away. He made a quick decision and began kicking off his boots. Seeing this, Mercer knew what was coming and charged forward. Making a dive for the outlaw, he caught the man just as he was going over the side. "No you don't," said Mercer, as he dragged the struggling man back aboard.

Then Sibeck was alongside again, and it was all over.

With the net boat in tow and the netters sitting dejectedly aboard the Rainbow, Sibeck headed back for the net. Mercer did the honors of pulling the net aboard, during which time he gained a new respect for the hard work involved in commercial netting. Half of the net— the part that Coito had not yet pulled—contained a large number of salmon, and Mercer was amazed as he pulled the big fish aboard, one after the other. With the net aboard, Sibeck set a course for Pittsburg.

When the case came to court, Demetras and Coito were charged with illegal gill-netting and possession of overlimits of salmon. The wardens offered into evidence the twenty-one net-marked king salmon seized from the Demetras' boat, thirty-four more salmon recovered from the abandoned gill net, and the net itself. In addition, the wardens estimated that Coito had thrown overboard at least fifteen other fish. All in all, it was a great case, and the two suspects were promptly convicted. Both received heavy fines and lost all their equipment. In addition, the two netters lamented the loss of one of the finest catches of salmon they had ever taken. The fish would have been worth a small fortune.

*   *   *

Mercer's last Delta patrol involved an unscheduled two-day stakeout of an asparagus shed near Rio Vista.

He and Sibeck had received a tip that a large load of stripers was to be hidden in the shed, and they made a quick decision to pick a hiding spot nearby and wait the situation out. Unfortunately, Mercer wasn't prepared for such a lengthy wait, and he suffered terribly from the cold. The load of stripers never arrived, and on this occasion Mercer didn't get his man. What he did get was a serious case of pneumonia that put him out of action for weeks.

As it happened, this was not only Mercer's last Delta patrol, but his last patrol as a member of the Flying Squad as well. The strain of the constant traveling and the long absences from his home were creating serious problems for him with his family. He therefore decided to look for a transfer back to a regular warden's position.

His promised promotion to captain hadn't worked out. He had again fallen victim to politics, and whoever it was who made the final decision on the captain position probably chose to go along with a candidate less outspoken than Mercer.

At the time, there were only two vacant warden positions that he would consider: an opening in Alturas—an area he knew well—and another in Chico. Mercer would have preferred the Alturas district, but his wife and daughter wanted to live in a less remote area. So this time the family won out, and in late April of 1938, after only one year with the Flying Squad, Mercer packed up and headed for Chico.

Snake

Near midnight, one cold, clear, December night, in the riceland southwest of Chico, a mud-spattered, black sedan crept slowly along a rutted country road. It traveled without headlights, the driver relying instead on the soft light of a three-quarter moon. Upon arriving at an intersection, the vehicle came to a stop and a lean figure stepped from the passenger side.

The man was of medium height and slim build, and was dressed in heavy hunter's clothing. Though it would have been difficult to spot in the moonlight, there was something unnerving about his appearance—something vaguely reptilian in his thin features.

Stepping quickly to the center of the intersection, the man peered off into the distance, his sharp hunter's eyes searching for headlights or other signs of human presence. Satisfied that he and his companions were alone, he began to listen, cupping his hands to his ears and turning slowly to scan in all directions.

Suddenly he stopped, listening hard to the south. A brief smile crossed his lips as he detected a faint but unmistakable sound. To the untrained ear, it could have been the far off rumble of a waterfall or perhaps a freight train grinding along in the distance, but Norman

Nicholas McVey, or 'Snake,' as he was known, knew exactly what it was.

Snake McVey had been born and raised in the grain country of the north valley, and as he stood there in the moonlight that brisk night during the winter of 1937, he knew he had found what he had come looking for. He recognized the faint, ominous roar he could barely discern to the south, as a large concentration of feeding ducks—ducks by the tens of thousands. He knew also that those ducks meant dollars in his pockets, for Snake McVey was a market hunter—a destroyer of wildlife on a grand scale, and as ruthless and destructive a poacher as the state would ever produce.

Seconds later, Snake, his driver, and a third individual, peering from the back seat, were southbound from the intersection, moving toward the ducks. A mile farther on, they stopped to listen again. The roar was louder now. A turn to the east soon brought them as near to the feeding birds as they could approach by car. Snake and his two companions stepped out to study the situation.

A quarter mile from the huge mass of ducks, the noise level was high enough to render conversation at normal levels impossible. The overall sound was still something of a roar, but at a quarter mile, the calls of the various species could now be identified. The dominant sound was the high-pitched fluting of multitudes of pintails, punctuated often by the sharp, descending rasp of hen mallards. Plus, there was the odd quail-like whistle of the wigeons. Behind it all was the continuous, grinding chatter always present with large numbers of feeding ducks.

Snake studied the flock for about ten minutes. He knew that flocks of feeding ducks are seldom stationary, but move slowly across the fields. Birds to the rear are constantly taking flight to move to the front of the mass. The ducks that Snake was watching, therefore, appeared to 'roll' slowly across the fields in leapfrog fashion, feeding as they progressed. By watching where airborne birds were landing, Snake was able to determine the direction of travel of the flock.

He determined also that the great flock was approaching a drainage ditch that bisected the rice field in which it was feeding. To Snake, the ditch was important, because it would provide an avenue by which he could approach the birds from cover. He glanced over at the moon. At least an hour remained before it would slip behind the coast range mountains to the west, leaving the valley in darkness and silencing the feeding ducks. Conditions could not have been better.

But there remained one thing to be done. The three men got back into the car and made a systematic search of the area surrounding the ducks. They had to be certain that the area was free of game wardens—or 'coyotes,' as wardens were known among market hunters. When satisfied that they had the night to themselves, they returned to the road near the ducks, at a point near the drainage ditch.

Snake stepped out and removed a battered Browning 'humpback' semiautomatic shotgun from behind the seat. While rough on the outside, the thirty-inch-barreled weapon was mechanical perfection on the inside, clean and well oiled. Then, from an elongated pocket sewn inside his canvas coat, he removed a foot-long steel tube that was the same diameter as the Browning's magazine tube. It was welded closed at one end, and contained its own spring, and its open end was tapped to receive the threaded end of the Browning's magazine. After removing the magazine cap from the Browning, Snake fitted the magazine extension into place. The addition of this highly illegal accessory effectively doubled the shell capacity of the shotgun.

From another deep pocket in his coat he brought out a handful of red paper 12-gauge shot shells. With practiced efficiency, he slipped ten of these through the loading port of the Browning. He then jacked one shell into the firing chamber, the bolt closing on it with a loud, metallic clack. Finally, he added one final shell to the magazine, and the heavy weapon was fully loaded, holding eleven shot shells and containing a combined weight of nearly a pound of number six lead shot.

On the opposite side of the car, the third subject, a lean, ferret-eyed poacher by the name of Reggie Straight, had loaded his own extension-equipped Browning and was awaiting instructions from Snake.

From the back seat, Snake grabbed a string-tied bundle of a dozen burlap grain sacks. With these in one hand and his shotgun in the other, he stalked out into the moonlit rice stubble, with Reggie close on his heels. The driver then drove the car out of the area to wait and watch for wardens.

Reggie had to hurry to keep up with Snake, whose long strides made short work of the first hundred yards along the drainage ditch. The two men then stepped down into the empty ditch and covered the next hundred yards at a crouch. Now it was time for the work to begin. With the ducks less than two hundred yards away, the men had to get down out of sight and labor along on hands and knees, relying on the ditch banks to screen them from the now nervous ducks. They moved slowly and deliberately, careful to keep low to the ground, for if the ducks caught even a fleeting glimpse of any part of them, the wary birds would be gone. It was a time-consuming, painful process.

The act of sneaking up on and shooting into massed concentrations of waterfowl is known as 'dragging' or 'pulling a drag.' The technique is bread and butter to the market hunters, and Snake McVey had refined it to a science by the time he had reached his teens. Reggie was a relative newcomer to the game but was showing definite promise, having learned most of what he knew from Snake.

Snake left the bundle of sacks behind when he sensed he and Reggie were nearly close enough to shoot. From the near-deafening chatter of the birds, he judged that they were almost within range. There was no way, however, that they could risk even a quick glance.

They inched along further, more careful than ever, the din of the great horde of birds seeming to shake the ground. Then Snake stopped, sure that the ducks were well within range. The nearest birds on the edge of the flock would be within twenty feet of him now.

With the time at hand, the two men crouched on their knees and switched off the Brownings' safeties. They each took a deep breath and then, on Snake's whispered command, they rose swiftly on their knees, bringing the shotguns to their shoulders simultaneously.

The first shots boomed nearly together, catching the startled birds on the ground and cutting huge swaths through their dense numbers. Then, like a clap of thunder, a hundred thousand frantic wings beat the air as the entire flock took flight, their dark mass nearly blacking out the moon.

With practiced precision, Snake and Reggie tracked the rising birds with the heavy shotguns, blasting ragged holes in the mass with each well-placed shot. Like beats from a metronome, the shots rang out in practiced rhythm, each one raking scores of feathered bodies back to earth. Some ducks died instantly and fell like stones, while others spun from the sky on shattered wings. Still others, with lesser wounds, set their wings and sailed off to die slow deaths elsewhere.

Then all was quiet. The two men moved immediately into the field and began the task of throwing the dead birds into piles and running down the less mobile of the cripples. Snake retrieved the bundle of sacks and they began filling them with ducks. Each sack would comfortably hold about twenty-five ducks, which was about the same number that a good duck dragger could average with each shot during a drag.

They picked up nearly four hundred ducks that night, but the real tragedy was in the large number of wounded birds that were lost. These birds would crawl off, earthbound and helpless, to die days later from gangrenous wounds or the jaws or talons of some predator. It is a sickening fact that only about two of every three ducks brought down in a drag are recovered—the rest are wasted. For this reason, good game wardens reserved a special loathing for duck-dragging market hunters.

Nearly all the birds the two poachers recovered that night were plump pintails, the 'money' birds of market hunting. There were some mallards as well, also worth good money, but many wigeon and teal weren't even brought in from the field.

Since ducks killed in drags are almost always hit from behind as they climb up and away from the gunners, there are very few shot holes in their breasts, a fact that adds greatly to their value. In Snake McVey's day, 'dragged' pintails and mallards, simply gutted and unpicked, would bring thirty-five cents each in San Francisco. Picked, cleaned, and ready for the oven, they would bring seventy-five to eighty cents, and the down could be sold later for additional profit.

When the last of the ducks had been sacked and the sacks stacked along the ditch bank, Snake and Reggie hurried back to the road and were picked up by the vigilant driver. Their work for the night was finished. Hired 'haulers' would be sent in to take the risks of transporting the sacked ducks from the field to a hidden picking shed near Butte City.

*   *   *

The following afternoon, a rather plain but well-dressed woman drove her black sedan to the rear service entrance of a large Oakland restaurant. Two men in white aprons hurried out to meet her and removed two large suitcases from the trunk of the sedan. The suitcases were carried directly into the kitchen, where they were immediately opened. Each contained three layers of cleaned, plucked, pintail ducks packed in neat, white rows. The birds were carefully counted, and Mrs. 'Snake' McVey was immediately paid in cash. She then hurried on her way to catch the ferry that would take her across the bay to San Francisco, where another large restaurant was awaiting her delivery. She smiled to herself—it would be a profitable day.

*   *   *

Snake McVey and Reggie Straight had gotten away with it again: they'd pulled another successful duck drag and made some money. But about this time, unbeknownst to them, Warden Gene Mercer was transferring to the town of Chico in the north valley, and things were about to change—the risks involved in duck dragging were about to multiply drastically. Snake and Reggie were about to find out, as were a number of other serious poachers, that the good times of big-money duck poaching were behind them and their days as market hunters numbered.

Road Hunters

Warden Gene Mercer was on the prowl. Southbound on Seven Mile Lane, he traveled at a leisurely pace, learning the roads and studying landmarks, ever alert for violators. After only a couple of weeks in his new district, he was already getting a feel for valley patrol. So far, he loved it.

He slowed the patrol car as a brightly colored cock pheasant strutted onto the road ahead. It was beautiful in the morning sunlight, with its crimson wattles and white-banded neck. A few feet away, a pair of buff-camouflaged hens fed leisurely along the roadside like domestic chickens. At the approach of the patrol car, all three birds crouched low and slunk away into the roadside stubble, and Mercer was amazed at how they could disappear so completely in such sparse cover.

As he continued on his way, several more pheasants crossed the road, and there were still more visible in the fields. They seemed to be everywhere. He had counted more than a hundred of them in the fifteen minutes since he had left Chico. Prime bait for poachers, he thought.

Upon passing Pratt Grant Road, he suddenly pulled over and stopped. Something had caught his eye.

Grabbing his binoculars, he stepped out and walked back to the intersection. Nearly a mile to the east, a vehicle was coming his way. As Mercer examined it through his binoculars, his interest was further aroused by the way it was being driven. It wasn't tracking straight down the road, but wandering from side to side—one of the telltale signs indicating road hunters. And it was traveling at an unusually slow rate of speed, which was also suspicious behavior.

As the car drew closer, Mercer could see the driver and one passenger, both of whom appeared to be scanning the fields on either side of the road. Suddenly, the vehicle stopped and a gun barrel appeared out the right window. The barrel bucked sharply and three seconds later, the sharp report of the shot reached Mercer's ears. Then the door flew open and the passenger trotted out into the field and picked up something that Mercer was certain was a pheasant. The suspect tossed the pheasant into the back seat, climbed in, and soon the car was underway again.

Mercer, suddenly worried that the approaching violators would see his patrol car, looked over and found, to his satisfaction, that the vehicle was hidden by some high, roadside tules. It appeared that he could simply remain concealed where he was, and step out in front of the violator's vehicle as they reached the intersection. They would probably be too shocked to react, but if they tried to run, the patrol car would be nearby. Satisfied with his plan, he stepped down into a dry, tule-lined ditch that ran along the edge of Pratt Grant Road. It would only be a short wait.

Crouched in the tules, Mercer was soon able to make out the faces of the approaching suspects. They appeared to be young men in their late teens or early twenties.

As the vehicle slowed to approach the intersection, the suspects saw neither the concealed warden nor his patrol car. However, they *did* see another rooster pheasant in the field to the north. The driver carefully applied the brakes and the passenger again stuck his shotgun barrel out the window and fired. The pheasant, caught broadside by the deadly pattern, was struck down and lay quivering in the dirt. The shooter bounded from the car and ran out to retrieve it.

The driver, waiting in the car with the engine running, was so intent on watching his friend that he failed to hear the approaching footsteps to his left. But he whirled around at the sound of a voice.

"State game warden, young man. Turn off your engine."

The color drained from the driver's face at the sight of the stern-faced warden peering through his window. He was so stricken with shock that it was several seconds before he could either move or speak. He just sat there, gasping for breath and staring out at Mercer. Finally, he reached over feebly and turned off the key. In the meantime, the other suspect had returned with the pheasant, having somehow failed to notice Mercer until he was all the way back to the car. He froze at the sight of the warden.

"Why don't you step around here, young man," said Mercer, indicating the front of the car. Still holding the pheasant, the suspect complied. Then Mercer directed the driver to get out and join his friend.

"I'll need some identification from you boys," said Mercer, and the two suspects reached for their wallets.

After examining the two driver's licenses, Mercer walked back and looked into the car. He had expected to see a bird or two and was therefore astounded at the sight of a large pile of pheasants completely covering the back floor. He opened the back door and picked through the pile, counting seventeen roosters and two hens. He was shaking his head as he walked back to the suspects. This had to be a commercial operation— they had to be selling the birds.

The two suspects, while shaken at first, recovered their composure quickly, and when Mercer informed them that he was taking them immediately before Judge

Lehman in Durham, they turned to each other and exchanged knowing grins.

Judge Lehman was the local justice of the peace and held court in the living room of his home. Upon being taken before him, one of the two young poachers greeted him with "Hi, Uncle Will," and Mercer knew he was in for a bad day.

Both subjects pleaded guilty, and Mercer was appalled when the judge fined them a mere twenty-five dollars each. When they asked for a few days to get the money together, the judge granted them until the following Saturday. The same young poacher then replied, "Thanks, Uncle Will. I can sell enough pheasants by then to pay the fine." He then flashed Mercer an insolent smile as he left the room.

Mercer turned immediately to Judge Lehman and asked, "Judge, isn't that contempt of court?"

The judge, irritated by the question, answered simply, "The matter's been settled."

The judge followed Mercer out to his patrol car and took possession of the nineteen pheasants, telling Mercer that he would dispose of the evidence himself. Mercer then drove away in disgust, having experienced his first bitter taste of Butte County justice.

*   *   *

It was fortunate that Mercer arrived in Chico in the spring, for the spring months were the slowest time of year in the Chico patrol district. Most of the ducks and geese were gone, the winter salmon runs were over, and the deer were in poor shape after the lean winter months. This gave Mercer a chance to learn the district without any pressing patrol problems to worry about. By the end of his first summer there, he had learned where most things were in the district and had traveled and learned most of the important roads. As fall approached, he was ready.

With the coming of fall, one might have noticed in

Mercer a certain spring to his step that had been absent the month before, a certain lifting of his spirits . . . for fall is game warden weather.

Salmon Snaggers

The farm country seemed deserted as Warden Gene Mercer drove along, enjoying the first hour of what promised to be a fine fall morning. He had been out since well before daylight, patrolling the valley south of Chico. Westbound from the little town of Nelson, with the early morning sun to his back, he slowed to cross the bridge over Butte Creek. There he paused a few seconds to watch the salmon chasing each other over a riffle a short distance below the bridge.

It was the height of the salmon run, and Butte Creek, like all the rivers and creeks in the Chico district, was choked with the big fish. They seemed to be everywhere, thrashing and darting around in the shallow riffles, often with their backs above water. They were highly visible and highly vulnerable, the perfect target for poachers. And there was no shortage of poachers. They pursued the salmon day and night with pitchforks, spears, gaffs, nets, snag-hooks, rocks, clubs, guns, and even explosives. It was a tough problem for the wardens.

Although Mercer was new to the problem, he pursued the salmon poachers with a vengeance, working long hours on Butte Creek, the Feather River, Big Chico Creek, the Sacramento River, and dozens of smaller streams in the district. He would sneak up on the hot spots, watch the violators take a fish or two, then pounce on them. He would seize their gear as evidence, relieve them of their illegally-taken salmon, and escort them to the nearest judge.

Most of the poachers were just small-timers with a fish or two, but from time to time, Mercer would get lucky and stumble onto something better. Such was the case this morning on Butte Creek.

As he continued on across the bridge, Mercer glanced upstream to the north. At that instant, he caught a brief flash of reflected sunlight from something in a willow thicket on the west bank about a half mile up. Most people would never have noticed, but it got Mercer's instant attention.

He turned quickly to the north, dropping down off the levee onto a little-used dirt road along the willows between the west levee and the creek. Driving as quietly as possible, he crept along until he spotted two pickup trucks tucked away in the willows a hundred yards ahead. He then carefully nosed his patrol car into the brush and stopped. Grabbing his field glasses, he stepped out, eased the door closed, and continued on foot. Using the willows for cover, he made his way to a point near the pickups where he could see the water.

Butte Creek, in that part of the valley, averaged about thirty feet across, and at the point where the two pickups were parked, the stream flowed through a long, quiet pool. At the head of the pool, to Mercer's surprise, two men stood in the thigh-deep water, each manning one end of a long panel of chicken wire. Each end of the wire panel was secured to a pole, and the men had positioned the poles such that the wire was stretched across the upper end of the pool, forming a fish-proof barrier.

Twenty yards downstream, there were two more men, similarly positioned, but instead of chicken wire, these men were pulling a section of net, complete with cork floats and lead line. They were working the net slowly upstream, crowding the salmon toward the chicken-wire barrier, where a fifth subject was busily wielding a long-handled gaff, hooking the salmon and tossing the thrashing fish onto the bank.

Focusing his field glasses on the poachers, Mercer recognized all five of them immediately. There was Old Man Levenger and two of his sons, notorious poachers from Glen County, and—to Mercer's chagrin—the two Corbett brothers. The Corbetts were farmers from the Chico area who had often passed useful information to Mercer and had become valuable informants. But now they had stepped beyond the law themselves and were about to find out that the past help they had provided Mercer had earned only his gratitude and nothing more. They would receive no special consideration.

The salmon, sensing their peril, had begun to panic, darting around, frantically searching for a way out. One frightened silvery female actually swam up onto the bank, her momentum carrying her well away from the water, where she flopped helplessly. Then, a forty-pound hook-jawed male, swimming at top speed, struck the legs of the suspect with the gaff, nearly knocking him off his feet.

It was at this instant that Mercer walked out into view, and the fish-catching operation came to an abrupt halt. The violators froze, their shock plainly visible on their faces. The man with the gaff dropped the implement, while the others just stood there, no doubt wishing desperately to be elsewhere. One of the Corbett brothers blinked repeatedly as though in hopes that Mercer would disappear. The two younger Levengers briefly considered running, but thought better of it, aware that they had been recognized.

The Levengers grumbled and swore to themselves as they waded ashore, complaining over the prospect of another fine. The Corbetts were quiet and subdued, more embarrassed than upset.

Mercer was amazed at the number of salmon the

poachers had captured. The bank was littered with the big fish, more than seventy of them in all. He directed the suspects to load the fish into their own pickups, along with the net and the chicken wire, then he followed them to Judge Lehman's house in Durham.

Judge Leh·ıan, interrupted while working in his garden, sat in his overalls, peering over his glasses as the five salmon poachers pled guilty. He then dispensed a dose of his own peculiar brand of justice. After letting them off with what he termed the "minium" fine, which was the ridiculously low sum of twenty-five dollars each, he went on to order their net returned along with five salmon each. The remainder of the fish he retained, telling Mercer, "I'll dispose of the evidence myself."

For some unaccountable reason, the Corbetts chose to pay all the fines, and the Levengers, who had gotten off scot-free, were in high spirits, chuckling among themselves as they drove away. Mercer could barely contain his disgust. The Corbett brothers, however, were appropriately humble and left quietly. Mercer got into his patrol car and drove away, pained by the all-too-familiar ache in his stomach that he always experienced when a bad judge made a joke out of a good case.

Surprisingly enough, the Corbetts never seemed to hold their humiliating experience against Mercer. In fact, they continued being 'good cooperators,' providing him with excellent information for a good many years thereafter.

A Crooked Jury

Mercer's frustrating experiences in the Durham Court were by no means unique. Many of the state courts at that time were bad, with judges totally unsympathetic toward the Fish and Game Division. Not only were many *judges* unsympathetic, but often the local residents were just as bad. In fact, many people at that time saw no reason to have laws protecting anything as abundant as pheasants and ducks, and they resented the fact that there were wardens sneaking around enforcing those laws. Mercer received a bitter lesson in this shortsighted philosophy during his first jury trial in the Biggs Judicial District.

It started with a patrol of the farmland west of Biggs one afternoon, a few weeks prior to the opening of pheasant season, when his attention was drawn to a slow-moving sedan. Maneuvering to where he had a clear view of the vehicle, Mercer trained his field glasses on it, determined to watch it for a while. Suddenly, the brake lights came on and a shot was fired from one window. Then a passenger jumped out and ran into the field. Mercer could see the man bend down and do something with his hands, but he couldn't tell what the guy was doing. The man then returned to the sedan empty-handed.

This puzzled Mercer, and although he was sure he had witnessed the illegal killing of a duck or pheasant, he stayed back to watch a while longer. Soon the same thing happened again: the vehicle stopped, a shot was fired, and the same man ran out, did something with an object on the ground, then came back, again empty-handed.

The road at that point took a slight jog, which put the sedan temporarily out of sight behind a line of willows. Mercer took advantage of this opportunity and drove hurriedly to the spot where he had first seen the sedan stop. There, a few feet off the road, he found a brown paper bag tied shut with a rubber band. Inside was a freshly killed rooster pheasant. He left it there and rushed to the next spot where the sedan had stopped. There he found another rooster pheasant, again in a paper bag secured with a rubber band.

He then drove at a good pace until the sedan was again in sight, at which time he slowed down to tail it from a distance. He had decided to sit back and allow the poachers ample opportunity to thoroughly incriminate themselves before he moved in for the arrest. He shadowed them for the next half hour, witnessing them kill five more birds.

Then they turned around and started to backtrack, stopping often to pick up the brown paper bags along the road. Mercer got out of sight, allowed them to pass, then followed them over miles of back roads, a route which led them ultimately toward Biggs. He lost track of the number of times they stopped to pick up bagged pheasants, but when he decided to stop them, a few miles out of town, he was certain they had a carload.

The driver of the sedan became uneasy as the tiny image of a car appeared in his rearview mirror. He grew more uneasy when he realized that the car was overtaking him at an alarming rate. A few seconds later, it was right on his bumper and a red light appeared. He had little choice but to pull over.

Mercer stepped from the patrol car, walked forward,

and got his first look at Charlie Blagg and Donald Short, a pair of habitual violators with whom he was destined to tangle on a regular basis in the months to come. They had had a noteworthy pheasant shoot that day, and when Mercer counted the brown paper bags heaped in the back seat, they numbered thirty-seven, each containing a cock pheasant.

He seized the pheasants, a shotgun, and a .22 rifle, then took the two men before the justice of the peace in Biggs. They were arraigned and promptly pleaded not guilty, requesting a jury trial.

When the day of the trial arrived, Mercer had total confidence. His case against the two violators was rock-solid. After all, he had actually *seen* them shoot at least six pheasants, plus he had caught them red-handed with a whole carload full of the out-of-season birds. He felt that there was no way he could lose.

He was to find out, however, that he had lost already, long before he entered the courtroom. The evidence was heard simply as a formality, as the jury, several members of which were active pheasant poachers themselves, had already made its decision. Mercer couldn't believe it when the foreman of the jury announced the verdict of 'not guilty,' and he left the courtroom feeling as though he had been kicked in the stomach.

Outside, he was faced with the unpleasant chore of returning the rifle and shotgun to the two poachers who went out of their way to crow about their victory and make the experience as humiliating as possible for him. He took some comfort, however, in the knowledge that things had a way of evening out in the long run, and he knew that sooner or later the two obnoxious outlaws would pay. This proved to be correct, for a few years later he had the satisfaction of sending one of them to prison.

Not-So-Dead Doe

The coming of fall also meant an increase in deer-related problems. There were always hard-core poachers who would kill deer year around, but deer season, and the days and weeks immediately before and after deer season, seemed to stimulate otherwise law-abiding people into illegal hunting activities. Mercer therefore spent considerable time, much of it at night, prowling the mountains and foothills in search of deer violators.

One such patrol began one night around midnight when he awoke and was unable to go back to sleep. He tossed and turned for a while and then, giving up on getting further rest that night, he eased himself out of bed, dressed quietly, and slipped out into the night. Soon he was in his patrol car heading up the Skyway, the crooked road that snaked its way along the south rim of Butte Creek Canyon. The lava cliffs appeared black in the moonlight as he drove along, and occasionally he glimpsed, far below, the dark, twisting line that was Butte Creek. Winding his way higher into the foothills, he passed through the sleeping communities of Paradise and Magalia, heading north toward Inskip and the prime deer country beyond. If asked why he had chosen this particular area to work this particular night, he would probably have attributed his decision to a simple hunch. But in reality, it was a fine-tuned decision-making process—largely subconscious on his part—which took into consideration a wide variety of factors of which he was constantly aware. These included weather, time of year, time of day or night, phase of the moon, and thousands of miscellaneous bits of information acquired through years of experience. It was possibly more of an instinct than anything else, but whatever it was, it was well developed and well exercised in Mercer.

At about 2:30 A.M., while driving through a densely forested area a few miles south of Stirling City, he spotted the glare of headlights coming his way. Since it was an unlikely time of night for anyone to be out on legitimate business, he stopped his car, turned on his red light, and stepped out into the roadway with his flashlight.

The driver of the oncoming car had to brake sharply to avoid hitting the patrol car and the uniformed officer standing in his path. Mercer motioned for him to pull off on the shoulder, and the driver reluctantly complied. Mercer then walked up to the driver's window, training his light on the two subjects within.

"State game warden," announced Mercer. "Are you men coming from Stirling City?"

"No, sir, we started from Butte Meadows," replied the driver.

"Have you passed any cars? I'm looking for a gray sedan," continued Mercer, relying on the canned words he always used in these situations. But before the man could answer, there was a loud, thumping noise from the rear of the vehicle.

"What was that?" asked Mercer. "What do you have in the trunk?"

The color had drained from the driver's face, and, despite the early morning chill, beads of perspiration had appeared on his forehead. "That's just my dog," he replied, a slight quaver in his voice. He was now gripping hard on the wheel to stop his hands from trembling, trying desperately to appear unconcerned.

Mercer walked around to the rear of the vehicle.

"That's no way to treat a dog," he said. "Come on back here and open this."

The driver hesitated, then resigned himself to the inevitable. He stepped out and walked slowly to the rear, while his companion sat staring at the floorboards.

The thumping had become louder by then, and as the driver unlocked the trunk and pulled up the lid, he narrowly escaped being struck by the sharp, flailing hooves of a wounded doe. Beneath the doe, Mercer spotted the skinned quarters of what turned out to be two more deer.

The wounded animal had been shot near Stirling City and hurriedly stuffed into the trunk, unconscious and mistaken for dead by the two poachers. The driver now stood staring at the struggling animal, cursing his luck at having it pick such an unfortunate time to come back to life. Mercer dispatched the hopelessly wounded doe then loaded it, with the two other deer, into his patrol car.

The poachers, after only a few questions from Mercer, admitted everything, explaining that they had killed the first two animals late the previous afternoon at Snag Lake.

Mercer drove the two men, who identified themselves as shipyard workers from Oakland, to Butte County Jail, in Oroville. There they remained until the following day, when they were taken before the judge in the town of Paradise. There they pleaded guilty, and the Paradise judge, who took a dim view of outsiders poaching local deer, fined them five hundred dollars each and confiscated their rifles and spotlight.

A Tense Situation

Like the two Oakland shipyard workers, most poachers, once apprehended, were submissive and cooperative. This wasn't always the case. One evening, at a secluded deer camp above Stirling City, on the day before deer season opened, a routine situation turned nasty and Mercer found himself in a bind.

He had talked only briefly with the three hunters present in camp when he sensed something was amiss. While they were outwardly friendly, there was something slightly unnatural in their speech and actions, subtle clues that Mercer detected immediately. He continued his casual conversation with the hunters, his senses now on full alert, his eyes busily scanning every inch of the camp and its occupants. Suddenly he spotted what he was looking for.

One of the hunters, a tall, lanky individual with nervous eyes, shifted his feet uneasily as he felt Mercer's gaze lock in on his lower legs. The man looked down and cringed as he noticed the rust-colored smear of freshly dried blood on the toe of his left boot. Mercer shifted his gaze to the man's face, and as their eyes met, he saw the man's look of distress change to one of defiance.

"How did you get blood on you?" asked Mercer. "That's beef blood," answered the man, an edge to his voice. "I helped a guy butcher a cow this morning. Why, is there some kind of problem?"

"Just doin' my job," replied Mercer as he started to move through camp, looking for more signs of the deer that he knew was somewhere nearby.

He found it hanging from an oak limb in a stand of young trees a few yards behind camp. It was a small spike buck, unskinned, a stick propping the body cavity open for cooling. It was undoubtedly intended for camp meat. Walking back into camp, he confronted the three hunters.

"Well, I guess you know you're in some trouble," he said. "Which one of you did the shootin'?"

There was no answer at first, and Mercer noted, with some concern, that the three had been drinking. There was a half empty whiskey bottle on the table, and the men appeared to be getting more belligerent by the minute.

"We don't know anything about no damn deer," said the one with blood on his boots. ". . . and you don't have anything on us."

"I'll tell you what," said Mercer, "I can either cite whichever one of you killed the deer, or I can cite all three of you for joint possession and let a judge figure it out. Now which one will it be?"

Suddenly, the one with blood on his boots reached over and grabbed a rifle leaning against a tree.

"You ain't gonna do either one," he said, bringing the rifle to bear on Mercer's chest. "You better just get on out of here before you get hurt."

But Mercer stood his ground, and while looking the man square in the eyes, calmly explained to him the sad mistake he would be making by resisting arrest.

"You don't really think I'll just go away, do you?" said Mercer. "I'm gonna take care of this tonight . . . even if I have to call in the Marines. Now do yourself a favor and put down the gun."

Mercer was convincing, as always, and fortunately the armed hunter sensed that he was dealing with no ordinary man. After a few seconds of silence, he seemed to wither under Mercer's hard gaze, and turned and put the rifle aside.

"All right, it was me," he said. "I shot the deer." He then indicated the other two men and said, "These guys didn't have anything to do with it." From that point on, all three men were cooperative, even to the point of helping Mercer load the deer into the patrol car. Mercer picked up the rifle, unloaded it, and placed it in the back seat. He then directed the rueful violator into the front seat for his ride down the hill to Butte County Jail.

*   *   *

Mercer had been unarmed during the above confrontation. His pistol had been where he usually kept it, on the front seat of his patrol car. Wearing a sidearm was optional for wardens in those days, and Mercer just wasn't one for packing a gun. He preferred to leave his gun in the car and rely instead on his wits and his line of gab to get him out of trouble.

There was to come a night, however, when his life would be hanging by a thread, and he would deeply regret this practice.

Win a
Few . . .

During Mercer's early years in the Chico district, pheasant season consisted of a single weekend in November, with the bag limit set at two birds per hunter on each of the two days. Legal shooting hours were from 8:00 A.M. to 4:00 P.M., and with such highly restrictive regulations, violations were numerous.

One opening morning, while patrolling for early shooters, Mercer was flagged down by some hunters at the Estes Ranch, between Chico and Dayton. They stood with guns and dogs at their cars along the road, anxiously awaiting eight o'clock so they could begin their hunt. Because they were obeying the rules, they were understandably perturbed over a couple of hunters who had ignored the eight o'clock shoot time and were in the field, actively hunting, a full half hour early.

The two illegal hunters were walking a ditch nearly a half mile from the road, and as Mercer was studying them through his field glasses, two roosters got up. Mercer could plainly see both birds rocketing up and away from the hunter, but then both crumpled and fell as the men shot. He checked his watch; it was still twenty minutes to eight.

Since the illegal hunters were in open grain fields,

Mercer knew there would be no easy way to approach them from cover. He therefore returned quickly to his patrol car and swapped his uniform shirt and hat for some nonuniform hunter-type clothing that would be less threatening to poachers. He then started into the field with a shotgun and Old Duke, his Labrador. By playing the part of a hunter, he knew he would be able to work his way much closer to the violators before alarming them. Old Duke, nose to the ground, coursed back and forth in the lead as Mercer, looking like any pheasant hunter, steadily whittled away the distance between he and the suspects. When the suspects changed direction to hunt along a different ditch, Mercer also turned, putting himself on a collision course with the two men.

The suspects, who had been keeping a suspicious eye on Mercer from the time he left the road, were now getting nervous. Something wasn't right about this fast-walking hunter who was beginning to crowd them. Mercer was still seventy-five yards from the two men when they suddenly stopped, now certain that Mercer was no pheasant hunter. They spoke briefly to one another, then turned quickly to head back the way they had come.

Mercer pulled out his badge and called out, "State game warden, men. Hold it right there."

The suspects paused only momentarily to look back, then continued walking away at a brisk pace. Mercer yelled again for them to stop, but instead they broke into a run. He started after them at a trot, a comfortable pace that ate up the yards, but one he knew he could maintain indefinitely. He knew better than to burn up all his energy at the beginning of a chase.

But the suspects were not so smart. They squandered their strength right from the start, intent on putting distance between themselves and the warden. They increased their lead at first, but soon started to weaken. After only a quarter mile through the grain stubble, their breathing was coming in long, ragged gasps.

Mercer, on the other hand, was just getting warmed up. Soon he began to gain on the two men, noticing that one of them was definitely having problems keeping up the pace. Finally, when the two men realized they would not be able to outrun the warden, they slowed to a walk. When Mercer got to them, they had come to a full stop, thoroughly winded.

The older of the two suspects, who appeared to be near collapse, was a large, heavyset individual in his mid-forties, while the other was a tall, muscular youth in his late teens. From the bulk of their game bags, Mercer was certain that they had overlimits of pheasants.

"You're under arrest," announced Mercer. The two violators, chests heaving, too out of breath to speak, just looked at him through narrowed eyes. "I'll need to see your hunting licenses and pheasant tags," continued Mercer, but the suspects made no move to comply. As they gradually recovered from their exhaustion, Mercer explained that they would have to accompany him back to his car.

"We're not goin' anywhere with you," exclaimed the older of the two suspects, "and you're not man enough to make us!"

They then turned and started to walk away. When Mercer attempted to stop them, they whirled around, brandishing their shotguns threateningly.

Now, Mercer didn't have a cowardly bone in his body, but he was much too smart to start a fight that he couldn't win. In this case, he knew that it would be extremely dangerous to attempt to arrest the two armed and belligerent suspects by himself. At best it would turn into a wrestling match—one he would probably lose—and the potential was there for someone to get shot. He therefore chose to back off a ways and follow the suspects until the odds improved in his favor.

They had gone only a short distance before Mercer got the chance he was looking for. A pickup truck turned off the main road onto a nearby dirt road and passed only a couple hundred yards ahead of him. By urgently waving his arms, Mercer was able to catch the attention of the driver, who immediately turned off the dirt road and steered toward what appeared to be three hunters in some kind of trouble. Soon the bouncing vehicle lurched to a stop in front of Mercer.

Mercer was delighted when he recognize the two occupants of the pickup as the McNair brothers, Palmer and Kenneth, stout young men who worked for the landowner. Mercer explained the situation to the McNairs, both of whom were anxious to help. In the meantime, the two uncooperative violators had continued walking in the direction of their car, still several hundred yards away.

"I'm deputizing you two men to help me make this arrest," announced Mercer to the McNair brothers. He then directed them to raise their right hands while he swore them in. He and the two brothers then hopped into the pickup and drove over to the suspects, who were still hoofing it toward their car. When Mercer stepped out, backed now by his two burly new deputies, the suspects were more willing to cooperate.

"You don't have to make a big deal out of this," said the older and more talkative of the two. "We'll go with you. You don't need these guys to help you."

"You're a little late for that," replied Mercer. "You've earned yourselves a trip to county jail."

Mercer first relieved them of their shotguns and game bags, then verified that they did have two birds over the legal limit. He determined also that they had been trespassing. Upon identifying them, he was surprised to learn that they were father and son.

The father had become very vocal by then, begging for a break and promising never to do that kind of thing again. Mercer gritted his teeth in disgust, for it always annoyed him to hear violators cry when they were caught—particularly violators who had given him a bad time.

He loaded the suspects and Old Duke into the back

of the pickup and climbed in after them. The McNairs then drove them straight to the Chico police station, where the father and son poaching team soon found themselves behind bars. They were charged on a variety of counts, including resisting arrest, and Mercer was hopeful that the experience might discourage the boy from future illegal activities.

A couple of weeks later, both father and son were convicted in a jury trial and fined $350 each.

... Lose a Few

On another of Mercer's early pheasant openers, in '39 or '40, things didn't work out nearly as well.

It was the second afternoon of the two-day season, and Mercer was patrolling along River Road, near the Sacramento River, west of Chico, when he was flagged down by Fred Corbett, a local farmer in the area. Fred was one of the two Corbett brothers that Mercer had once pinched for netting salmon. Corbett reported that a party of five men had been hunting all day on the nearby M & T Ranch and had been doing a lot of shooting. He was certain that they had killed far too many pheasants.

Mercer drove immediately to a point along one boundary of the M & T to take a look. He soon spotted the hunting party spread out on either side of a small slough near one end of the ranch. They were hunting in the direction of a small airstrip. Each man carried a shotgun, and Mercer could catch an occasional glimpse of the pointers that were busily working out ahead, sniffing through the prime pheasant cover. Mercer noticed, through his field glasses, that the game bags of all five men appeared to be bulging with birds.

Corbett had told him that the main access to that

part of the ranch was a gate a half mile up the road. Mercer drove to it and found it to be locked. He had a ring of keys with him and spent a few minutes trying them in the lock, but he had no success. He then drove back to the spot where he could see the hunters.

While he had been at the gate, the hunting party had arrived at the airstrip, where a light plane was waiting. Then, as Mercer watched, a pickup pulled in with what appeared to be a huge pile of pheasants in the back.

"Probably yesterday's birds," thought Mercer, as he watched the hunters begin loading the pheasants from the pickup into the airplane. There were obviously far too many birds for the number of hunters present. Mercer was getting worried. He was not yet familiar with the roads and access points of the M & T Ranch, and he was faced with what was fast becoming an urgent situation. He quickly drove to another gate that he knew of, but it too was locked. He considered shooting off the lock, but decided against it—a decision he would later regret.

He then drove around to the back of the ranch to a point not far from the airstrip. He parked his car, climbed the fence, and started on foot toward the plane. He was well aware, as he jogged along, that there was no time to spare, for the loading of the airplane appeared to have been completed.

When he had only 150 yards to go, he became concerned over what appeared to be a ditch bank up ahead between himself and the airstrip. Just then, he heard the high-pitched whine of a starter motor and the aircraft engine coughed into life.

The plane was taxiing to the end of the airstrip as Mercer scrambled up the ditch bank and discovered, to his dismay, that he faced a long, deep stretch of Little Chico Creek. He searched frantically for a way across, but found nothing. He was about to jump in and swim across, when the pilot gunned his engine and began his takeoff roll. At that point, there was nothing Mercer could do but watch helplessly as the plane cleared the runway and gained altitude. And the evidence of what would have been a spectacular pheasant case disappeared into the blue.

He had failed. He should have shot the lock off the gate. His wrong decision had cost him the case and allowed several substantial violators to get away. But occasional failures were a part of the job—a painful part of the job—and good wardens learned to take their defeats in stride.

A week later, a ranch hand told him that the five hunters had hunted the entire weekend and had killed many times their legal bag limits of pheasants. Mercer had no choice but to chalk up the incident to experience.

The House on Stilts

Fred Corbett had just parked his tractor when he heard the shot off in the distance. And a few minutes later, when the old sedan drove by, he was certain that its driver had been the shooter. He watched the vehicle as it continued north on the River Road, its driver scanning the fields on either side of the road.

"Damn road hunters," muttered Fred, and then, on impulse, he climbed into his own car and started out to pursue the other vehicle.

The Corbett farm was situated on a large piece of fertile ground near the Sacramento River, west of Chico. Fred and his brother Dave, partners in the farming operation, had often been annoyed by illegal hunters who trespassed there to poach pheasants and ducks, and in recent years, they had been tipping off the local game warden.

Fred stayed well back, barely keeping the poacher's car in sight as it continued slowly up the River Road. Once, it stopped again, and although Fred didn't hear the shot, he was certain that there had been one. It was difficult to see at that range, but he was reasonably sure that he had caught a glimpse of the poacher briefly getting out of his car.

After crossing the bridge over Big Chico Creek, the poacher turned west onto a smaller road that led through a small forest of massive valley oaks to the Sacramento River, a short distance beyond. The road ended at a vast gravel bar that marked the confluence of the Sacramento River and Big Chico Creek.

On one edge of the gravel bar, on the north bank of Big Chico Creek, huge pilings had been driven into the ground. Perched on top of the pilings was a small house, its floor a good eight feet above the gravel bar, the rear of the rude structure actually extending out over the waters of the creek. It was to this elevated house that the poacher drove, and Fred Corbett, watching from a distance, observed the poacher carry something up the steps and disappear inside. Fred then turned around and made a beeline for the telephone back at the farm.

"Hello, Mr. Mercer? This is Fred Corbett ... I've got another one for you."

*   *   *

Mercer was well aware of the importance of informants. He knew, from his own experience, that tips he received from informants yielded at least 80 percent of his most important cases. He referred to his informants as 'cooperators' and actively recruited them throughout his district, encouraging them to act as eyes and ears for him.

The Corbett brothers were among Mercer's best cooperators, coming through with good information on a regular basis. So upon receiving Fred Corbett's report of a pheasant poacher at a house on stilts, he went to work getting a search warrant for the place.

Early the next morning, Mercer and Warden Earl C. Vale of Willows paid the pheasant poacher a visit. The wardens concealed the patrol car well away from the house and made a stealthy approach on foot. Vale waited out of sight below the house, while Mercer climbed the high, plank stairway to the front door. Halfway up,

Mercer saw the curtains of one window part briefly then heard rapid footsteps and some sort of commotion within. He reached the front door and knocked loudly. There was no response.

"State game warden ... I have a search warrant, now open up!" yelled Mercer.

Still no response. He was just about to kick in the door when the doorknob rattled and turned and the door opened a few inches. Mercer found himself staring up into the unfriendly eyes of a huge man with a sour expression.

"I have a warrant to search these premises," announced Mercer, holding up the document he had carried with him.

"My wife isn't dressed, you'll have to wait," growled the big man.

"Put her in the bedroom, I'm comin' in!" replied Mercer, and when the man made no move to comply, Mercer shouldered his way through the door, knocking him aside. Mercer turned, poised for battle, but nothing happened. The burly poacher just stood back and glowered at him. The man's wife, fully clothed, was at that moment hurrying in from the back porch, looking nervous and very guilty.

Warden Vale, waiting below, heard Mercer muscle his way in the door, and, almost simultaneously, he heard a loud plop in the water behind him. Turning toward the creek, he was in time to see a falling object hit the water, making a second plop. Hurrying to the bank, he used a long stick to fish in two rooster pheasants floating on the surface.

Mercer had explained the reason for his visit, and both husband and wife were in the process of denying any knowledge of any pheasants when Vale showed up with the two sodden birds that had miraculously fallen from the sky. This brought the conversation to a close.

After a quick search, in which the wardens failed to uncover any additional evidence in the house, Mercer questioned the man and his wife. The poacher then grudgingly admitted to shooting the birds, and his wife admitting tossing them off the back porch. Mercer scribbled out a quick citation while Vale secured the man's shotgun into evidence. Then, with their business completed, the two wardens went on their way.

Waterfowl Problems

The valley portion of Mercer's Chico patrol district was centered squarely in the great waterfowl migration route known as the Pacific Flyway, and for five or six months of every year it was winter home to millions of ducks and geese. They came in vast flocks that darkened the skies, and they brought with them a good many headaches for the game wardens charged with protecting them.

Mercer soon learned that the most serious poaching problems he faced in the Chico district concerned waterfowl—and the most determined and destructive of the waterfowl poachers were the professional market hunters. Market hunting was big business in the thirties and forties, and there were a dozen or so infamous market-hunting families operating within a thirty-mile radius of Chico. Men like Snake McVey and Doby Dick Pruett made thousands of dollars each winter killing ducks and selling them to the big hotels and restaurants in San Francisco and Oakland.

For the wardens, market hunting was an extremely difficult problem to deal with. As a group, market hunters were cunning and resourceful, and they took remarkable precautions to avoid arrest. For instance, the men who did the actual shooting, known appropriately as 'shooters,' rarely came out of the field with ducks. The job of getting the ducks from the field, into a vehicle, and then to a hidden picking shed—the riskiest task of all—was usually left to hired 'haulers,' quite often juveniles. Then there were 'drivers,' who not only drove for the shooters, but acted as lookouts as well. And, of course, there were the 'buyers,' who provided the market for the birds.

The shooter was the most important member of the market-hunting team. His task was to crawl to within a few yards of a flock of ducks and kill as many birds as possible before they flew out of range. This required stealth, steady nerves, and considerable skill with an extension-equipped shotgun. There was a certain amount of prestige in being a shooter, and the best among them were regarded as genuine celebrities in some communities. They were judged by the average number of ducks they could bring down with each shot during a drag, and the best of the shooters could average more than forty birds per shot. It was therefore possible for a single shooter to personally account for as many as four hundred ducks in a drag, and there could be as many as four shooters firing at once.

To prepare the ducks for sale, most market hunters only gutted them and sold them, feathers and all, for about thirty-five cents each. Toward the end of the market-hunting era, in the early fifties, unpicked birds sold for as much as a dollar each. A few market hunters, however, like Snake McVey and the Blagg brothers, took the trouble to pluck them, and, in doing so, more than doubled the sale value of the birds.

It's not hard to see why market hunting—which even in the thirties offered potential profits of between $100 and $250 a night—was so common at the time. But it couldn't go on forever, for it was having a disastrous effect on waterfowl populations. Old-time valley wardens, who had once looked upon waterfowl as being an inexhaustible resource, were beginning to feel uneasy as they noted fewer and fewer returning ducks and geese each year. The accepted method for catching market hunters, or waterfowl draggers in general, required the warden to first locate a large flock of feeding ducks, then 'sit on 'em.' If the warden got real lucky, which happened relatively infrequently, the shooters would choose that particular flock, and pull the drag right in front of the warden. Even then, unless the warden was close enough to actually see the shooters fire or gather up birds, it was tough for him to put together a case that would stand up in court.

It was much more common for the wardens to catch the haulers. If a warden was close enough to hear the drag, and was able to locate the dead birds between the time the shooters left and the haulers arrived, he could capture the haulers in the act of bringing out the birds.

Most market hunters preferred moonlit nights for their illegal forays. The ducks tended to be actively feeding and noisy in the moonlight, which made the big flocks easier to locate than on dark nights, when they were sometimes totally silent. For this reason, wardens' night stakeouts on flocks of waterfowl would usually last until the moon went down. Wardens referred to this as 'putting 'em to bed.'

Mercer was not altogether new to 'workin' ducks' when he arrived in Chico. Like most mountain wardens, he had gone on several waterfowl assignments in late fall to Tule Lake, the great gathering place of migrating ducks and geese on the California/Oregon border. He would travel there at the close of deer season to help the local wardens control the multitudes of duck and goose hunters that converged on the area. The assignment would last until the big freeze, usually in November, when the lake would ice over and send the millions of ducks and geese winging their way south to the warmer, feed-rich Sacramento Valley.

When the waterfowl left Tule Lake, many mountain wardens were sent out of the hills to help the valley wardens deal with their waterfowl problems. In the northern Sacramento Valley, these wardens stayed at what was known at the time as 'the duck camp.'

Located about two or three miles east of Maxwell, the duck camp was a bunkhouse complex that could accommodate up to a dozen men, including a full-time camp cook. As many as eight wardens at a time stayed at the duck camp and worked at catching waterfowl violators, their main targets being the market hunters. Wardens sent to the duck camp could plan on spending the entire winter there, getting only a little time off at Christmas. Mercer got stuck with the assignment only one winter, in about 1934, but he made the best of the experience and learned a lot about waterfowl.

The duck camp was a good idea, for it not only placed increased enforcement pressure on the important problem of market hunting, but it provided some relief from the boredom experienced by mountain wardens during the slow winter months.

Four and Twenty Blackbirds

Ducks, geese, and pheasants weren't the only targets of market hunters during the early years of Mercer's career. There were a few serious commercial hunters who specialized in hunting blackbirds. While not as profitable as duck dragging, blackbird hunting offered one major advantage: it happened to be legal.

Redwing and Brewer's blackbirds were common in the north valley, and they often occurred in dense flocks of more than a quarter of a million birds. These flocks, which appeared as black clouds in the distance, could be seen for miles as they descended on grainfields like swarms of locusts.

A stealthy hunter who worked his way close to such a flock could empty his shotgun into it and kill upward of five hundred birds in a matter of seconds. He would then spend the remainder of the day gathering them up, gutting them, and stringing them, a dozen at a time, on wires or willow switches. These were later sold in the Bay Area for thirty-five to forty cents a dozen. The buyers, usually of southern European extraction, would then transform them into a variety of savory old country dishes.

One day, during Mercer's only winter at the duck

camp, he was sent out by the cook to shoot something for dinner. He encountered a large flock of blackbirds, and with a single 12-gauge blast of number nine shot, he knocked down more than a hundred of them. Back at the duck camp, the cook, Clarence McDonald—known to the wardens as 'Old McDonald'—baked them into a pie. Mercer claimed it was delicious and described the blackbirds as tasting every bit as good as doves.

Duck Drag

Mercer was fortunate, during the first few years following his transfer to Chico, to have the help of an outstanding assistant warden by the name of Garrie Heryford. Heryford, a tall, good-natured, well-proportioned young man with blond hair and sharp blue eyes, worked in fish hatcheries during the spring and summer months, but was assigned to assist Mercer the rest of the time. With a great thirst for adventure, Heryford was one of the few men who could match Mercer's enthusiasm for warden work, hour per hour. In addition, he had the sharp wits and imagination found in only the best of wardens. He and Mercer were inseparable during the winter months of the early forties, and together they made a formidable team.

One afternoon, following an unproductive all-night stakeout of an unusually large bunch of ducks, Mercer and Heryford returned to the area they had left early that morning to see how the enormous flock had fared during the day. Mercer's mother, who had come to live with Mercer and his wife, was along for the ride, as was Heryford's wife. The two wardens thought it would be nice to show the ladies what a flock of half a million ducks looked like.

Shortly before dusk, they turned west off Highway 99, just south of the town of Nelson. Arriving in the area where they had spent the previous night, the wardens were disappointed to find that the birds had moved. But Mercer pulled over to look and listen, and he soon had the flock located again, a mile farther west.

He was about to start the car to drive for a closer look, when he suddenly froze, listening hard to the west. From the direction of the ducks came a rapid, popping sound—a series of distant shotgun blasts, the unmistakable sound of a drag. All eyes turned to the flock of ducks as it lifted skyward, an ominous black cloud, sounding much like some huge swarm of angry insects. It was an awesome sight, one the women would not soon forget.

Mercer quickly slid from behind the wheel, then spoke hurriedly to Heryford.

"Take the women back to town, then come back and meet me at the bridge," he instructed, reaching back through the window for his binoculars. He then turned and set out at a trot toward the scene of the drag. Behind him, Heryford spun the car around and raced away toward Chico.

As he ran, Mercer replayed in his mind the sound of the drag. There had been more than twenty rapid shots.

"Probably three shooters with magazine extensions," he thought.

Then he recalled the steady, businesslike rhythm of the shooting.

"Definitely not amateurs," he concluded, amazed at their audacity to pull a drag during broad daylight.

There had been no shooting after the initial rolling volley, another sign of professionals. Less-experienced violators would have been running around shooting cripples, and Mercer was certain that the field would be alive with injured birds. But there was no shooting. The violators would take no further chance of alerting any wardens that could be around.

Mercer was jogging along easily when he spotted a car coming in his direction from the area of the drag. Fortunately, the bridge he had mentioned to Heryford was only a short distance ahead, and he was able to sprint to it and conceal himself as the vehicle approached. The bridge spanned a drainage canal, and the area between the bridge abutments and the water provided good cover. Peeking out carefully from his hiding spot, and with the aid of his binoculars, he was able to determine that the driver and sole occupant of the vehicle was a woman.

"Probably makin' a dry run to see if I'm around," thought Mercer, as the car rumbled across the bridge and continued eastward toward the highway. It hadn't gone far, however, when it turned around and started back. Then, to Mercer's dismay, it came to a stop in the center of the bridge, and the driver cut the engine. He heard the door open, then dainty steps on the rough planks above his head. He froze in alarm as feminine legs appeared, stepping carefully down the bank.

The woman, although certain that she was totally alone, had apparently chosen to play it safe—to get out of sight beneath the bridge to answer nature's call. She hummed softly to herself as she went about her business, totally oblivious to the horrified game warden cowering in the shadows less than ten feet away. Then a few seconds later she was gone . . . and Mercer relaxed with an audible sigh.

The woman started the car and headed back toward the scene of the drag, and Mercer was fairly certain that when next she came his way, the shooters would be with her, with a load of ducks—or so he hoped. Mercer was in a good spot, for the road dead-ended to the west just beyond where the shooting had occurred, and the poachers would have no choice but to come right by him when they attempted to leave the area.

It was dark when Heryford returned with the patrol car, creeping along without lights. Mercer, expecting the duck draggers at any second, quickly explained to

Heryford his plan for a head-on stop of the violators a short distance beyond the bridge. Heryford would stay in the patrol car, concealed behind some willows, until Mercer signaled. Mercer would be up ahead, seventy yards or so, and would flash his light briefly in Heryford's direction when the time was right.

They had barely worked out the details on their plan, when headlights appeared to the west. Mercer ran quickly ahead and concealed himself in a roadside patch of tules as Heryford backed off the road into his assigned position. Then they waited, pulses pounding, vaguely aware of the curious tightness in the chest that always seemed to accompany the last few seconds preceding an ambush.

The headlights seemed to grow larger as the vehicle approached, and to Mercer it seemed to take forever to arrive. Then it passed him, and he pointed his light at Heryford and gave it two quick flashes. Heryford responded immediately; the patrol car seemed to leap onto the roadway, engine racing, lights ablaze.

The poacher's vehicle halted instantly, halfway between the two wardens, as Heryford bore down on it from ahead, and Mercer sprinted after it from behind. Mercer arrived at the driver's door as Heryford skidded the patrol car to a stop, nose to nose with the other vehicle.

The stop had been executed flawlessly, but the poachers, veteran violators, were not the type to give up. The doors on the right side of the vehicle flew open and three dark figures jumped out and made flying leaps into the canal that paralleled the road. They were already scrambling up the opposite bank when Heryford cleared the driver's door of the patrol car and jumped in after them. Mercer had no choice but to stay with the vehicle to ensure that the driver—the woman he had observed earlier—didn't take off with the evidence.

Heryford had wasted no time in getting after the suspects, but they had had too much of a lead on him. By the time he thrashed his way across the canal and made it up the far bank, the three men had disappeared into the night. He had no choice but to return to the road, sopping wet and badly frustrated.

Mercer was far from being pleased with the way things had worked out, but at least they had the car and driver, plus he had gotten a good look at one of the poachers. The one in the front seat had been illuminated for one brief instant by Heryford's headlights, before he jumped out and ran. Charlie Blagg's sinister face was a hard one to forget, and Mercer had recognized him instantly. Blagg, with whom Mercer had tangled before, was reputed to be one of the worst of the north valley's market hunters. He would be picked up later, definitely a good catch.

Mercer's black mood lightened perceptibly when the woman, not yet recovered from the shock of capture, identified herself as Stacy Blagg, Charlie's wife. And Mercer was further cheered by the discovery of all three extension-equipped, long-Tom shotguns in the back seat—shotguns that had seen their last duck drag.

The trunk of the vehicle was stuffed full of ducks, more than a hundred of them, and while they were only a fraction of the birds that had been killed in the drag that evening, they represented irrefutable, damning evidence against the Blaggs.

Bringing ducks with them in the car had been a foolish risk. The Blaggs had been careless, and now they would pay the price. And the following morning, Mercer and Heryford would increase this price by finding a few hundred more ducks in sacks at the scene of the drag.

Stacy Blagg ended up spending the night in Butte County Jail, and she entered a not-guilty plea in the Durham court the following morning. Her husband Charlie, who had undoubtedly shared a chilly walk home that night with his two companions, was picked up by Mercer on a warrant a day or two later. Mercer was almost certain that the two who got away were Edward Blagg, Charlie's brother, and Donald Short, another of

Mercer's past customers. But he would have to wait for another chance to catch these two.

Mercer was expecting the worst when the Blagg cases came to trial, for he had had a long series of unpleasant experiences with Butte County juries. But when the day arrived, he was amazed at the outcome: it took the jury only a few minutes to find the Blaggs guilty of all charges. Apparently the jury, which was composed of farm-country men and women who would normally have condoned a certain amount of game poaching, felt that the Blaggs were getting much too greedy. Mercer was then further amazed when the judge imposed a sentence that one could have expected had the three hundred or so illegally killed ducks been the judge's personal pets. While Stacy Blagg got off with a mere hundred dollar fine for her part as the driver and lookout, her husband Charlie received a month in county jail and a five hundred dollar fine.

"That ought to slow him down," thought Mercer, as he walked from the courtroom. But time would prove this bit of speculation to be far from the truth.

Burned Out

By around 1940, with a couple of years in Butte County behind him, Mercer had made quite a name for himself. He had rampaged through the problem areas of his district, arresting poachers by the dozens, and the outlaw community was having to sit back and admit that the good old days were probably gone forever. The increased risk of arrest was taking a lot of the fun out of poaching, and many of the less serious violators were simply giving it up. Mercer seemed to be everywhere, and many violators had already experienced their second arrests by Mercer, and some even their third.

George Eggert, a thief and general ne'er-do-well of Chico, was among the unlucky few who had run afoul of Mercer on three separate occasions, the last having occurred during one of his foraging raids to the valley. When he visited an unattended barnyard and supplemented his bag of out-of-season pheasants with several domestic ducks and geese and a sixty-pound pig, Mercer had seen it all and had run him down. For Eggert, getting caught the third time wasn't pleasant, but enduring the frequent ribbing he had been receiving ever since from his motley collection of friends was far worse. Still, George Eggert wasn't the type to spend a lot of time being mad . . . he was the type that got even.

One night in a poker game, in a smoke-filled gaming room in south Chico, Eggert was doing some thinking. When the subject of his most recent arrest was brought up, and as he sat glowering while a half dozen of his half-drunk companions shared a round of raucous laughter at his expense, he made a decision. Referring to Mercer, he was heard to say, "Well, I'll get that son of a bitch, I'll burn him out."

There were several men present that night who recalled those words when the following evening Mercer's house mysteriously burned to the ground.

Mercer had been working with Taylor London in Colusa County, and happened to be at London's home when the call came in.

"Your house blew up," advised the excited telephone operator, who hastily added, "but nobody was hurt."

She then went on to inform Mercer that his family had been taken in by friends. Mercer was grim-faced as he slammed the receiver down, ran to his car, and sped off toward Chico.

Arriving at what had once been his home, he was stunned to find absolutely nothing left. Only a pile of smoldering rubble remained to mark the spot. He stared in shocked disbelief at the remains of everything he owned—clothes, furniture, photographs, personal records—everything gone.

When investigators probed through the charred ruins, they found the electrical fuses unblown, a fact which they felt ruled out an electrical fire. Searching further, they eliminated the other common causes of house fires. In the end, they concluded that the blaze was most probably the result of arson.

When pressed by investigators as to what could have caused an explosion in his garage, Mercer remembered a barley sack that had contained three large, explosive rocket flares known among wardens as 'duck bombs.' They were military devices intended to be fired from mortar tubes, but the wardens had learned to launch them from sections of well casing. When launched, they would streak skyward, trailing smoke and fire, until they exploded violently in dazzling bursts of burning magnesium. They were unreliable, dangerous things, but were very useful for scaring ducks away from roads or driving them from rice fields.

The duck bombs in Mercer's garage went off well after the fire started, having been ignited by flames, but many of Mercer's neighbors were of the mistaken belief that the explosion had preceded the fire. At any rate, the destruction of house and garage was complete.

When advised the following day of George Eggert's threat, Mercer seethed with rage, but resisted the immediate urge to go gunning for the man. He went instead to the insurance company and gave them the information. Although highly interested in the story, and despite a thorough investigation, the insurance people were never able to pin the blame on Eggert. But Mercer had no doubts as to Eggert's guilt, and for weeks he wrestled with the temptation to confront the man. He knew, all too well, however, that any retaliation on his part would probably cost him his job, a fact that probably saved Eggert from grievous injury.

Goose Drag

During the months preceding World War II, Mercer was occasionally visited by his old friend Gene Durney, who by that time had been promoted from assistant warden to full-time warden in charge of the Sacramento arm of the Flying Squad. One November evening, during one of these visits, the two men were out on foot east of Butte Creek, keeping watch on a large grind of geese that was working in on the Adams Ranch.

It was just past sunset, and the huge flock of feeding snow geese appeared as a solid white blanket in the rice stubble a mile east of the ranch headquarters. A closer look revealed the presence of dark geese as well— white fronteds, known as 'specks' among hunters, and stately Canadas. The flock contained no fewer than ten thousand geese, their combined voices audible for miles, and more were arriving each minute. There were swarms of them in the twilight sky above the flock, circling lower and lower, many with wings set, gliding in gracefully to land gently among the others. The two wardens looked on with genuine appreciation, reveling in sights and sounds of which good wardens never tire.

It's not surprising that they failed to notice the four dark figures, bearing shotguns, that were crawling up on the geese from the west, staying low behind the rice checks. The wardens' first indication that something was amiss came when the huge flock suddenly exploded into flight, an awesome sight. The roar of the wing beats and multitudes of frantic voices arrived a couple of seconds later, accompanied by the popping sound of a ragged volley of shotgun fire.

Mercer and Durney glanced quickly at one another, then set out at a brisk walk for the spot nearly a half mile to the south. Several minutes later, they climbed over a wire fence that enclosed a large expanse of rice ground more than a mile across. By then they were close enough to barely make out the silhouettes of the four men, three hundred yards ahead in the dwindling light. But there was something else—the wardens paused to look and listen, for something was going on up ahead that was definitely out of the ordinary.

The hunters were scurrying around, apparently gathering dead and wounded geese and throwing them into a pile. But there was a sense of frantic urgency in their actions that puzzled Mercer, until he saw one of them run over and kick at the dark silhouette of something that responded with a piercing, high-pitched squeal. Then the wardens could make out other low, shadowy forms darting here and there, apparently in competition with the men over the geese. More animal grunts and squeals followed, mingled with angry shouts and curses of the men. "Hogs," uttered Mercer, as he and Durney started forward again.

It was the practice at that time for farmers to run hogs on their harvested grainfields, for hogs could do well on grain missed by the harvesters and could be sold later for a nice profit. It was in one of these fenced grainfields containing hogs that the goose drag occurred that November evening in 1941.

Mercer and Durney were able to approach the hunters unnoticed, for the men were totally occupied in their battle to save the geese they'd killed from nearly a hundred highly aggressive, hungry hogs, many of which weighed well over three hundred pounds. It was complete pandemonium, with the men yelling and kicking at the foul-smelling creatures that grunted and squealed furiously, crazed by the smell of fresh blood. Here and there, hogs could be seen chasing down and fighting over crippled geese, ripping them to shreds, while others—the more bold among them—were charging in past the hunters to snatch geese out of the pile.

One of the hunters was engaged in a tug-of-war with a large sow that had her jaws clamped to the other end of the goose he was carrying, when he looked up and saw the wardens only a few yards away. The sow took advantage of his surprise, jerked the goose from his grasp and ran off with it, snorting triumphantly. The other three hunters noticed the wardens at about the same time.

"State game wardens," announced Mercer, displaying his badge as Durney did the same.

Then came the tense moment as the wardens awaited the reaction of the illegal hunters. Would they run or fight? As it happened, they did neither. While obviously not pleased at being caught, they cooperated—a decision that saved them a night in jail. Mercer, despite the fact that he had never seen a more wasteful violation, decided to let the hunters off with citations to appear the following morning in the Durham Court.

Mercer wrote furiously, attempting to get all four citations written before the last dim glow of daylight departed. Durney, in the meantime, was engaged in an epic battle with the hogs. The animals had converged on the pile of dead geese, and despite Durney's best efforts, they were gobbling the birds down at an alarming rate.

"Here now . . . get away, damn you . . . hold it, there . . . ." cried Durney, as he ran around the dwindling pile of geese, kicking frantically at the crazed hogs.

Mercer looked up briefly from his writing and noted, with scientific interest, that a large hog could wolf down a medium-size goose—guts, feathers, and all—in little more than five seconds. It was not a pretty sight, a clean white snow goose disappearing into the foul pig jaws, with the accompanying grunts and snorts, and the revolting nightmare sounds of crunching bones and tearing flesh. Mercer gave an involuntary shudder.

He finished the last of the citations and sent the violators on their way, then turned to Durney who was wielding a dead goose, flailing wildly at a large boar with it. The boar retreated a few feet then stood, popping its jaws menacingly.

"We've got to get these geese out of here," cried Durney as Mercer waded into the melee.

Both wardens then grabbed as many geese as they could carry and headed out, stumbling through the darkness toward the nearest fence, some two hundred yards to the east. Unfortunately, their car happened to be parked at the ranch headquarters, a mile in the opposite direction. Upon reaching the fence, they threw the geese over and headed back to the pile for more. They had no trouble finding their way back, guided by the frightful feeding sounds of the hogs.

Kicking and pushing their way back through the frenzied animals, both wardens were acutely aware of the dangers they faced. Hogs were dangerous animals at best, but these half-wild, blood-crazed creatures could become man-killers at any second. To slip and fall among them would certainly prove fatal. The wardens hurriedly grabbed up another load of geese and started again for the fence. By then, it had started to rain.

It took seven or eight hazardous round trips and the better part of an hour for the wardens to carry the remaining geese through the muddy rice ground and get them over the fence. On the final trip, most of the hogs followed, squealing and grunting in hideous chorus, nipping and snapping at the geese the wardens carried. When the men at last reached the fence, they heaved the geese over, then hastily clambered over after them, collapsing, exhausted, on the wet ground.

When they recovered their strength, they found

themselves facing the dismal prospect of carrying what turned out to be 142 dead geese over the mile and a quarter of rain-muddied road, in almost complete darkness, back to their patrol car. The 142 geese represented only about half the birds that had been brought down in the drag, the hogs having eaten the rest.

Since the roads were soaked and in bad shape, there was no hope of driving the car out to the geese, so they had no choice but to pick up all the geese they could carry and start walking. They carried the geese out in relays, a job that took them all night. It was daylight when they stuffed the last goose into the back of the patrol car, and a short time later it was time to meet the four violators in court.

The court proceedings took place in Judge Lehman's living room, and the matter took only a couple of minutes to decide—which was a good thing, for otherwise Mercer and Durney would probably have fallen asleep. The four men pleaded guilty and Judge Lehman, as Mercer predicted, fined each of them the minimum twenty-five dollar fine and announced that he would personally dispose of the evidence. Mercer looked over at Durney, who slowly shook his head in disgust.

Outside, as Mercer and Durney unloaded the geese onto the judge's front lawn, His Honor came out of the house to take a look. He picked up a goose, held it up, and upon examining the bird, he assumed a sour expression and exclaimed, "What? They haven't even been gutted?"

The mud-spattered, bone-tired wardens just glowered at him for a second or two, then turned and got into the patrol car and drove off.

The Undertaker's Ducks

Warden Gene Durney found himself in Butte County again during the spring following the goose case on the Adams Ranch, in which he and Mercer had nearly become hog bait. He was in Chico on Flying Squad business, working on a Butte County outlaw, Earnest Bertoli, who had been selling game. Bertoli had been a problem for a long time, always involved in some kind of shady dealings, most of which involved illegally taken game. Durney had been in town only a short time when he learned that Bertoli had sold some out-of-season ducks to a local undertaker. Durney wasted no time in getting this information to Mercer.

A short time later, Mercer pulled up in front of the Shady Oaks Mortuary, a somber-looking structure which occupied a well-manicured corner lot near the center of town. It was owned and operated by Alfred D. Malloy, undertaker, known to many as 'Digger.'

Digger Malloy was nowhere in sight as Mercer entered the mortuary office, but a young woman was seated behind a desk in one corner.

"May I help you, sir?" she asked, eyeing the Fish and Game patch on Mercer's uniform.

"I'm here to see Mr. Malloy," Mercer replied.

The woman hesitated, and Mercer was sure he caught a flicker of alarm in her eyes.

"I think he's down the hall in the chapel," she said, pointing to a doorway on the opposite side of the room. Mercer thanked her and headed down the hallway.

The cool air in the chapel was heavy with the sweet, florist-shop smell emanating from a dozen or so large floral arrangements positioned around an open casket near the altar. Mercer looked around. The sole occupant of the chapel was the occupant of the casket, and a quick glance satisfied Mercer that it was not Digger Malloy.

Back in the office, there was another door that led down a stairway to a large basement. When Mercer returned to the office, the young woman was just coming up from the basement, looking nervous and upset.

"Is he down there?" asked Mercer, but the look on her face was enough. He hurried past her to the stairs and started down.

Digger Malloy, a thin, nervous man, stood fidgeting near the bottom of the stairs, doing his best to appear unconcerned. Behind him was a wall of refrigerated vaults.

"I understand you just bought some ducks," said Mercer, seeing no reason for preliminary small talk.

"Ducks? No, not me. I've never bought any ducks," he said, shifting nervously from one foot to the other.

"Well, how did you get duck feathers all over you?" asked Mercer, certain that he had interrupted the man in the process of picking the ducks.

Malloy looked down and winced at the sight of the bits of feathers and duck down adhering to his wool shirt, but he came right back with a reply.

"These must have been left over from duck season," he said, brushing vigorously with both hands at the front of his shirt.

But Mercer was by then following a trail of feathers that appeared to lead to one of the vaults. As he approached it, Malloy stepped in front of him, saying,

"You can't look in there. Do you have a search warrant?"

"Stand aside, Malloy," said Mercer. "This isn't a private dwelling . . . I don't need a warrant."

Malloy hesitated, then stepped back, certain that Mercer would look in the vault one way or another. Mercer then pulled open the vault, the big drawer rumbling out on its runners. It was more than six feet long, designed for the cold storage of human bodies, but in this case, it contained about a dozen plump mallard ducks. Several of the birds had been freshly plucked.

Mercer held one of the birds up and turned to Malloy.

"Were you gettin' ready to embalm 'em?" he asked. But he received no reply. Digger Malloy sat dejectedly on the bottom step of the stairway as Mercer wrote out the citation. Mercer didn't consider Malloy much of a violator, but he couldn't have people buying ducks and creating a market for the likes of Bertoli. Mercer had hoped that Malloy would admit to buying the ducks from Bertoli, but Malloy—obviously afraid of reprisals from Bertoli—wouldn't talk. Mercer didn't press the issue, but allowed Malloy to sign the citation. He then gathered up the ducks and went on his way.

A Deal for the Chief

Shortly after the undertaker case, Mercer got word that Bertoli was at it again. This time he was reported to have sold a quarter of out-of-season venison to the chief of police of one of the larger towns in Butte County. This put Mercer in a highly uncomfortable position, for the chief of police was very popular in the community, and to arrest him would win no friends for Fish and Game. It would also surely embarrass the police department and possibly alienate the police officers against wardens.

The Chief wasn't really dishonest—at least not in the eyes of most people at that time. There was a prevailing attitude in those days that Fish and Game laws were somehow made to be broken, and to do so was in no way a negative reflection on one's integrity. While the Chief would never have considered accepting a bribe or taking something that wasn't his, he was known to bend the game laws now and then, and he openly condoned this type of conduct among his police officers. Actually, he never really thought much about his occasional wanderings beyond the limits of Fish and Game law, but when Mercer caught him cold with the illegal venison, the subject suddenly got his full attention.

Knowing there would be no chance for a search warrant—the Chief being a close friend of the local judge—Mercer had gone to the Chief's home and confronted his wife while he was at work. The Chief's wife had proven to be totally cooperative and had led Mercer to a back room where the meat was stored in an ice box. Mercer took the meat with him, and headed for the police station.

"You've got me in a hell of a spot, Mercer," said the Chief, with visions of scandal and disgrace running through his head. "Do you know what this is going to do to me?"

"Well, you've been asking for this for a long time," replied Mercer, not fully pleased with the situation himself. He wasn't overjoyed with the prospect of a feud with the police.

"Couldn't you just let it go this time?" begged the Chief. "I'll give you my word that it will never happen again."

Mercer was thinking. There was something worrying him about this case; something beyond the unpleasant prospect of hard feelings between him and the the police. It had to do with the deer meat—something didn't look quite right about it, and he decided to postpone any action against the Chief until the meat could be analyzed.

"I'll tell you what," said Mercer. "I'm going to think this over, and I'll get back to you."

"I'd really appreciate it," said the Chief, still greatly troubled, but relieved that Mercer hadn't proceeded immediately with a formal complaint.

It took more than six weeks to get back the lab report on the meat. During this time, Mercer stayed away from the Chief, and the Chief—figuring no news was good news—made no attempt to contact Mercer. When the report finally arrived, Mercer's suspicions were confirmed. The technicians at the Strawberry Canyon Lab had identified the meat not as venison, but as goat meat. The Chief was off the hook.

It was disgusting news for Mercer, for the Chief had thought he had purchased a genuine quarter of venison. The man had fully intended to break the law, and it was only through a stroke of incredible luck that he had been swindled by Bertoli and sold goat meat for venison.

In view of the Chief's intentions, Mercer saw no reason to inform him of the lab report. Instead, Mercer met with him, and told him "Chief, I've decided to give you a break ... provided, that is, that you promise to change your ways and obey the Fish and Game laws."

The Chief, who had been expecting the worst, relaxed with a sigh of great relief. He agreed readily to Mercer's terms and thanked him profusely.

"I owe you one, Mercer, and I won't forget it," said the Chief sincerely as Mercer was walking out the door.

"You don't owe me a thing," replied Mercer over his shoulder, thinking wryly to himself that he'd never spoken truer words.

*   *   *

In the meantime, Durney had been working hard to build a good case against Bertoli. He had infiltrated the crowd that Bertoli hung out with, and he had accumulated enough incriminating evidence against the man to make a good package for the district attorney. But it wasn't to be. Shortly before Durney was to make his move, Bertoli was arrested for passing bad checks and was sent to state prison. Durney had to return to Sacramento with very little to show for his two weeks in Butte County.

Rocket Attack

At the outbreak of World War II, many of the younger state wardens ended up in the military service. This left the remaining warden force spread pretty thin. Gene Durney and Garrie Heryford both joined the military, as did several other north valley wardens. Mercer was in his forties by then, and although he volunteered, he was never called to go.

To fill the void left by Garrie Heryford, Fish and Game assigned another assistant warden, Rudy Gerhardt, to assist Mercer in Butte County. Gerhardt lived in Gridley and worked with Mercer off and on during the war years.

Gerhardt, born in Germany, had immigrated to this country at age twelve, and being a native-born German, the war years were not easy for him. His situation was complicated by the fact that his mother had been a housekeeper at the German embassy prior to the war. But Gerhardt was tough, ignoring the frequent verbal abuse—he was often referred to as 'the Nazi'—and Mercer found him to be excellent help. He was good company as well, an intelligent, good-natured officer with a well-developed sense of humor—the latter being a trait that sometimes got him into trouble.

One cold night, in a rice field west of Biggs, Mercer

and Gerhardt sat bundled up in the patrol car near a large flock of feeding ducks. They had been there almost nine hours, since sunset, hoping for a duck poacher to liven the evening. But they had had no such luck. And now they watched as the last bit of moon disappeared behind the Coast Range Mountains. It was still a couple of hours until dawn, but with the valley in darkness, the ducks had become silent and would now be in little danger.

"Well, that's it for tonight," said Mercer, as he started the patrol car and headed east toward Gerhardt's car, parked a short distance out of Biggs.

Gerhardt said very little on the way back, unusual behavior for him, but Mercer just figured he was tired. After all, it had been a long, uneventful night. But Gerhardt wasn't overly tired; he was deep in thought. In fact, he was plotting a devious prank against Mercer, and he smiled to himself as the idea developed.

"See you tomorrow," said Mercer as Gerhardt stepped out of the patrol car.

"Good night, Saber," returned Gerhardt.

Having dropped Gerhardt off at his car, Mercer turned around and started north toward Chico.

Gerhardt, chuckling to himself, hurriedly popped open the trunk of his car and withdrew a grain sack containing a single rocket flare. Squat and ugly, the device was a dangerous and notoriously unpredictable piece of military ordnance of the type wardens referred to as a duck bomb. Working swiftly, Gerhardt then pulled out his duck-bomb launcher—a two-foot-long length of well casing welded to a stand—and placed it on the ground. Sighting along the tube, he quickly aimed it in the direction of Mercer's disappearing taillights. He then tittered and tee-heed as he slid the duck bomb down the throat of the launching tube. By this time, he was so racked with mirth that he had difficulty applying a lighted match to the fuse. But it finally ignited with an angry hiss. He scrambled away, giggling merrily, to watch from a distance. If all went well, the projectile would pass over Mercer's car and explode somewhere in front of him, giving him a good surprise. It would be a fine joke.

But this particular duck bomb had spent several weeks bouncing around in the trunk of Gerhardt's car, which had done nothing to improve its aerodynamic qualities, and when it fired, it did a number of things that were definitely not included in Gerhardt's plan.

There was an initial puff of smoke and a tiny spurt of flame that was just enough to pop the rocket out of the tube and onto the roadway. It lay there smoldering menacingly for a second or two, then went off with a roar. Without the launching tube to guide it, it began spinning and hopping around furiously in a cloud of smoke and fire. Terrified, Gerhardt dove headlong into a ditch and peeked out just in time to see the berserk missile skip along the roadway and lodge in the undercarriage of his patrol car.

"Oh no! Oh no!" screamed Gerhardt, eyes wide, both hands covering his ears.

The car lurched as the bomb detonated with an ear-splitting blast, sending shards of white-hot magnesium streaking in all directions. A piece or two of the burning metal struck Gerhardt, who jumped up yelling and beating wildly at his clothing.

Finally, when it appeared that he was no longer on fire, Gerhardt walked over to survey the smoking remains of his patrol car. It seemed to sag dejectedly on injured wheels as he approached, but upon closer inspection, he found, to his surprise, that it wasn't quite as bad as he'd thought. The engine block had absorbed much of the blast, but still, everything on the front half of the vehicle that wasn't made of iron or steel—this included wiring, hoses, distributor cap, etc.—had been torn loose or blown into small pieces.

Twenty minutes later, the phone was ringing in Mercer's home as he walked through the door.

"Hello, Saber?" asked Gerhardt. "Ya, it's me," replied Mercer.

"This is Rudy. My car won't start," said Gerhardt, condensing a lot of information into a simple, undeniable statement.

Mercer sighed and said "All right, I'm on my way." He hung up and started wearily out the door.

Gerhardt was waiting, sheepishly, a tow rope already attached to his car, dreading the explanation that he was sure Mercer would demand. But to his relief, Mercer was too tired to ask questions. He just hooked the tow rope to his vehicle and climbed back behind the wheel, anxious to get the task out of the way so he could go home and get some sleep.

"Thanks, Saber," said Gerhardt, as Mercer left him and his disabled car in front of his little house in Gridley.

"Don't mention it," replied Mercer, as he drove away.

It was several weeks before Gerhardt finally got up the nerve to admit to Mercer what had really happened. Upon hearing the truth, Mercer roared, thinking it was the funniest thing he'd ever heard.

Fatal Error

In addition to duck bombs, the wardens had access to another useful piece of military equipment, the Vary pistol. Looking like a six-gun from a cartoon, the Vary pistol was equipped with an enormous barrel of comic proportions. The pistol broke open at the breech to accommodate a huge flare shell roughly two inches in diameter and five inches in length. The Vary pistol could fire a projectile several hundred feet into the air, where it would burst, releasing a bright-colored flare that would descend slowly beneath a silk parachute. Like duck bombs, Vary pistols were useful for herding ducks and other wildlife from planted fields.

But Vary pistols, like duck bombs, could also be highly dangerous. They were subject to misfires and would occasionally hang fire (a hang fire occurs when the firing pin makes contact with the cartridge's primer, but ignition and explosion of the charge is delayed). A hang fire is extremely dangerous to the shooter, particularly if he opens the breech too soon. Such a mistake could easily prove fatal.

The U.S. Fish and Wildlife Service supplied Vary pistols to the state wardens during the thirties and early forties. Most wardens in agricultural areas had several of the things on hand to sign out to farmers with problems concerning birds or animals damaging their crops. The warden would leave the Vary pistol and some flare shells with the farmer and then return for it a few days later. But the warden would always make sure the farmer was aware of the hazards involved in using the things. This practice of loaning the farmers Vary pistols continued until an unfortunate accident in the north valley put an end to it.

Mercer had been approached by a farmer who had a problem with bandtail pigeons raiding his fruit orchard. The farmer, a Dutchman in his early twenties, had recently emigrated from Holland and lived with his wife and young child on a small farm south of Chico. Mercer signed out a Vary pistol to him and gave him a lecture on its use, stressing the dangers of opening the device if it misfired. The man nodded often in apparent understanding. But he somehow failed to get the message, for shortly after Mercer left, he did exactly what the warden had warned him not to do.

When several hundred bandtails returned that afternoon to his fruit trees, he loaded the Vary pistol to scare them off. Pointing the pistol skyward, he braced himself and pulled the trigger. Nothing happened. Having expected a heavy recoil, he was surprised when there was only the metallic click of the firing pin. But a tiny spark had been struck and was struggling for life within the shell.

Puzzled, the young man disregarded Mercer's warning and thumbed the breech lock. The barrel broke forward and down, revealing the wide brass base of the shell, which the young man eyed curiously. The shell chose that instant to explode.

There was a loud bang, followed by the thump of the Vary pistol striking the ground. The young man staggered backward, then fell heavily, half his face torn away. He was dead when his wife got to him a few seconds later, his blood soaking into the rich earth he had come halfway around the world to farm.

Shortly after this terrible incident, the U.S. Fish and Wildlife Service collected all the Vary pistols and the state wardens no longer had access to them.

As could be predicted, a lawsuit against Mercer and the U.S. Fish and Wildlife Service was filed, and the deceased farmer's wife, a native Chico girl, was awarded a substantial out-of-court settlement.

Stakeout

It was cold and dark and wet and miserable — and Warden Gene Mercer was having doubts. He peered with weary eyes at the spot of yellow light where an electric bulb cast its glow on the front porch of a large, ramshackle house some one hundred yards distant. It was a market hunter's house, reported to be a storage place for illegally killed ducks bound for sale in the city. But Mercer, after seven long hours, had seen neither ducks nor market hunters. Despite his boredom, he stared with complete concentration, studying the old house as though willpower alone could bring about some action—anything to break the monotony of the long December night. But all was quiet.

Huddled nearby, Warden Taylor London was also feeling the numbing effects of the stakeout they had begun shortly after dark. Now it was after midnight, an icy rain had begun to fall, and the two wardens were discovering that the ruins of the old shed they had chosen for their vantage point were offering poor shelter from the weather. London shivered and pulled his turned-up collar closer to his ears.

"I guess it isn't gonna happen," he said. He was beginning to doubt the information he'd received the previous day from a paid informant—information that had brought him and Mercer to this run-down neighborhood on the outskirts of Colusa.

"They should've been here by now," London continued. "Maybe they're stuck or broke down or somthin'."

"Let's give it another hour," said Mercer.

Veterans of hundreds of cold stakeouts, the two wardens were no strangers to boredom and discomfort, and they could stick it out, regardless of rain or cold, for as long as necessary. But tonight their information wasn't panning out. The informant had been certain that the three commercial shooters would be back from their illegal foray well before midnight, but it hadn't happened. It was a puzzling thing, for the valley was thick with huge flocks of wintering waterfowl. It should have been easy for the poachers to shoot a pickup load of ducks. So why hadn't they come?

It was 1943. America was at war, and many of the younger California game wardens were away in the service. This left the older wardens to fight the local battles against game violators. Gene Mercer, at forty-two, and Taylor London, a year or two younger, were among those left behind to 'mind the store'—and the 'store' couldn't have been in better hands. Mercer, London, and a handful of other dedicated wardens were working marathon hours, seven days a week, making life miserable for game poachers. The market hunters, being the most destructive of the game poachers, were feeling the brunt of the wardens' efforts, and very slowly, the wardens were gaining the upper hand.

Mercer turned, for the hundredth time that night, to look down the dirt road toward the duck country. There had been no traffic on the road all evening, but this time, car headlights appeared, coming his way. The vehicle slowed as it approached the driveway, then turned in and stopped in front of the house. Three men emerged, each bearing a shotgun, climbed the front steps and went inside. The wardens watched carefully, straining to see if there were any indications that the men had brought game with them. There were none.

The wardens were certain that the men had been hunting, and with waterfowl so numerous, they had undoubtedly killed ducks. The question was, were the birds in the car in which the men had arrived, or were they still in the field? Odds were on the latter. If so, someone would be going after the birds later—either the same three men minus their shotguns, or possibly other men hired as 'haulers.'

Another anxious hour passed as the wardens awaited further developments. Then finally, at about 2:00 A.M., the three men emerged from the house, without their shotguns, and left. Two of them took the car they had arrived in, and the third man took a second car that had been parked near the house. The wardens were intrigued by the suspects' use of two cars. Could it be that they were going after a load too large for one vehicle? It was two more bone-chilling hours before the wardens got their answer.

They waited.

"Here they come," said Mercer, jumping to his feet. He pounded his gloved hands together to get the circulation going as the headlights drew near. As the two vehicles turned into the driveway, the wardens sprinted to some shrubbery that offered a closer view of the house. They were wet to the skin and half frozen, but their discomfort was now totally forgotten.

The three men stepped quickly from the cars and opened the trunk lids. In the dim glow of the porch light, the wardens could make out a large mound of feathered bodies in each trunk. The men immediately began unloading the freshly killed ducks onto the porch, and they were so involved in this task that they failed to notice the dark forms closing in on them from two sides.

"State game wardens, hold it right there!" thundered Mercer.

One startled outlaw rose up abruptly and crashed his head on the trunk lid, while another just stood frozen in his tracks. The third man hesitated only briefly then bolted, running smack into London who quickly subdued him with a bear hug. Then it was over, and the wardens herded the poachers onto the porch and into the light. There the offenders stood quietly, fumbling for their driver's licenses, slightly nauseous with the realization that they'd finally been caught.

Although the suspects were in hand, caught with a massive overlimit of ducks, the wardens weren't finished. London's informant had stated that there were already ducks at the house—ducks killed the night before and possibly stored in a hidden room. The house would have to be searched.

A middle-aged woman had come to the front door in time to see her husband arrested, and she stood sullenly in the doorway as Mercer approached.

"Ma'am, we're going to have to see in the house," said Mercer.

The woman looked over at her husband. The man reluctantly nodded his consent, knowing full well that the house would be searched whether he liked it or not. The wardens then directed the three men inside to sit at the kitchen table while they made their search.

It wasn't a huge house, but rooms had been added and it was a rather confusing layout. The wardens first made a cursory search of the various rooms, with special attention given a spacious pantry and some large closets. But they found nothing. There was a ladder leading up to a sizable attic filled with old furniture, trunks, and boxes—but no ducks. The wardens went through the house again, this time with extra care, searching for evidence of a hidden room. Still no luck.

Then Mercer's sharp eyes were drawn to a small, rust-colored spot on the wood floor. Was it dried blood? A closer look revealed other spots in a barely visible trail that led from the front door to one bedroom. There the trail disappeared under a large rug which covered the bedroom floor. London folded the rug back revealing not only more blood spots, but one corner of what appeared to be a trapdoor in the floor.

The two wardens moved the bed aside and folded the carpet all the way back. The trapdoor was hinged and equipped with a steel ring that folded flush with the floor. London grasped the ring and tugged the door open, revealing a dark chamber with a ladder descending into it.

Back in the kitchen, the man of the house was holding his head in his hands and swearing softly. He hadn't expected the hidden basement to be found. Now he was *really* in trouble, facing a possible stay in the federal penitentiary, for the federal judges had no sense of humor when it came to market hunters.

Mercer eased his way down the ladder into the darkness, where he located a light switch. London looked on expectantly as Mercer snapped on the light and looked around. Then Mercer looked up and gave London an affirmative nod. Their search was ended.

A short while later, London was focusing his flash camera on about two hundred ducks that had been killed and hidden the day before. There were sixteen strings of about a dozen birds each, hanging in a row, suspended from an overhead beam of the basement ceiling. When combined with the ducks the three men had killed earlier that night, the total added up to close to five hundred illegally taken birds.

There were indications that the market hunters had been operating for a long time. Mercer noted old drippings on the basement floor—evidence that attested to the fact that ducks had been hidden there many times in the past. He examined the shotguns that had been used—semiautomatics with well-worn magazine extensions. There was no question that the three men were big-league poachers.

It took about an hour to wrap things up. The wardens took more photographs, loaded the ducks and the shotguns into London's patrol car, and advised the poachers of their pending date with a federal court judge. The poachers were looking grim when the wardens finally drove away.

On his way home that morning, Mercer was well pleased with the work of the previous night. He knew that even the best wardens, despite their best efforts, usually caught only the more careless of the poachers. It therefore felt particularly good to catch some smart ones for a change.

As Mercer drove along, pleasant visions of stern judges and jailed market hunters occupied his mind. Then he was home, and his thoughts turned to more immediate things—game warden luxuries like a hot shower, dry clothes . . . and maybe even a little sleep.

A Spy Named Sour-Wine

If there was ever a turning point in the wardens' war against market hunting, it came in the early forties as a result of a single case made by Mercer and Rudy Gerhardt. It was a good case in itself, involving the arrests of some particularly troublesome commercial hunters, but it also set in motion a series of events that would later prove to be devastating to *all* market hunting in northern California.

It happened one gray winter afternoon, late in 1943. Mercer and Gerhardt had located a huge flock of ducks resting in a field just north of the Biggs Afton Road, one of the main country roads running east and west across the valley. About a quarter mile east of the ducks, the road crossed Cherokee Creek, a stream bordered by high flood-control levees. The two wardens were in position on the Cherokee Creek levee a short distance south of the bridge. It was an elevated position from which they could watch the ducks and await developments. Their patrol car was stashed in an isolated barn a half mile to the west.

They were so intent on watching the thousands of ducks, and the noise generated by the birds was so intense, that they failed to notice the approach of a black sedan which came up behind them from the direction of Biggs. Mercer cursed to himself at being caught out in the open, but to his surprise, the three occupants of the car somehow failed to see him and Gerhardt, apparently intent on watching the ducks. As the car rumbled across the bridge, Mercer was certain he recognized Charlie Blagg among the passengers. The vehicle continued west, paused briefly near the ducks, then continued on.

Things suddenly looked more promising for the morning. Mercer felt certain that Charlie Blagg and his friends weren't just out to enjoy the scenery, and if they decided to pull a drag on the ducks, he and Gerhardt would be in an excellent position to catch them. Mercer wasn't concerned when the vehicle went on past the ducks, for he was reasonably certain that Blagg would return after searching the area for wardens—a search that was going to turn up nothing.

Then something occurred that was totally unrelated to Blagg and the duck drag, but that put the wardens in a better position to handle what was to follow.

About halfway between the wardens and the flock of ducks, a dirt road known as Wickman Road intersected the Biggs Afton Road from the north. As the wardens watched, scanning the miles of grain stubble for any sign of Blagg and his friends, they suddenly heard the unmistakable sound of .22 rifle fire coming from somewhere up Wickman Road. There were willows and high tules along the road, but with the aid of their binoculars, the wardens could see the top of a car that was stopped on the road about three-quarters of a mile north of the intersection.

The wardens quickly left the levee and ran to the intersection, where they could see the car to the north traveling slowly in their direction. As they watched, the car stopped, a gun barrel appeared out the driver's window, and a shot was fired. The driver then jumped out, ran into the field, and retrieved what appeared to be a pheasant.

Mercer instructed Gerhardt to wait at the intersection, then set out at a trot to get the patrol car. It took him only a few minutes running west down Biggs Afton Road to get to the barn where the vehicle was hidden. During this time, his eyes were never at rest as he jogged along, keeping a sharp watch out for Blagg. He was certain the outlaw would return.

Mercer was now directly south of the ducks, the closest birds being less than two hundred yards away. There were more than a hundred thousand of them on the ground, chattering noisily, with more birds arriving each minute. The overcast sky was full of them, circling and descending in small flocks, gliding in on cupped wings to finally flutter down among the others.

Mercer got to the patrol car and started back to Gerhardt's position, but as he approached, Gerhardt signaled for him to hold back. Mercer waited a few seconds, then Gerhardt signaled him to come on in. The poacher had just shot another pheasant. Mercer picked up Gerhardt at the corner, then turned north onto Wickman Road. The startled pheasant poacher had nowhere to go as the patrol car bore down on him, its red light glaring. He could only pull over and await his fate.

The wardens made short work of the case, anxious to send the poacher on his way and hide the patrol car again. Mercer scribbled out the citation as Gerhardt hurriedly recovered a half dozen pheasants from the vehicle, all shot with the .22 rifle. Mercer glanced around often as he wrote, afraid that Blagg would show up and see them. After a record-quick explanation of the citation and the court date, Mercer handed his pen to the poacher and directed him to sign.

Mercer had just given the pheasant poacher a copy of the citation when suddenly, to the west, the great flock of ducks erupted into flight. The flock lifted skyward with a thunderous roar, but not so loud as to drown out the rapid booming of shotgun fire. And it was close, less than a quarter mile to the west.

The two wardens and the pheasant poacher looked on, spellbound. The dense cloud of birds gained altitude and appeared to rain ducks as the gunners continued their deadly work. Hundreds of birds tumbled from the sky as load after load of lead shot sliced through the flock. Then it was over, and Mercer was vaguely aware of a sickening ache in the pit of his stomach.

In game-warden work things rarely go exactly right. It is seldom easy to catch serious poachers, for there always seems to be one or more problems concerning terrain, visibility, or distance that help poachers and hinder wardens. But on this day in 1943, everything came together for the wardens. Their arrest of the pheasant poacher had, by pure accident, placed them in perfect position to go after the duck draggers. Not only were the wardens close, but their patrol vehicle was parked against some willows and out of sight of the poachers, and they weren't far from a drainage canal that extended west directly into the area of the drag. The canal had high banks, with enough tules and willows to conceal the wardens in their approach. Everything was in their favor.

The wardens quickly sent the pheasant poacher on his way, then started down the canal bank, working their way toward the outlaws. They had to pick their way through the heavy foliage, keeping low to stay out of sight.

Before long, they could hear voices ahead. Mercer crawled up the bank, where a peek through the tules revealed two men, heavily loaded with ducks, trudging along the canal in his direction.

"Perfect," thought Mercer. His luck was holding. The poachers were even on the same side of the deep canal that he and Gerhardt were on. The two wardens then burrowed into the tules beside the path the poachers would walk. The voices grew louder, and the wardens waited silently, adrenaline flowing, poised for action. In less than a minute, the poachers were upon them.

Mercer was the first to move. Waiting until the lead

man was only a few feet away, he burst from the tules in front of him.

"State game wardens ... you're under arrest," announced Mercer, as Charlie Blagg let out a strangled cry of surprise and recoiled a step or two. Blagg didn't resist, knowing instinctively that he couldn't escape.

But the reaction of the other poacher was instantaneous. With remarkable speed, he darted through the tules on the canal bank and leapt into the water, ducks, shotgun, and all. Then, abandoning these things, he struck out swimming for the opposite bank.

But Gerhardt was ready for him. The warden launched himself in pursuit like a sprinter out of the blocks, crashing through the tules to spring like a cat from the bank. He landed squarely on the man's back. There followed a violent thrashing and splashing which lasted for a half minute or so, until Gerhardt emerged, dragging the half-drowned poacher behind him.

Mercer recognized the man immediately as Lester Bates, one of the more infamous commercial gunners in the area. The man offered no further resistance, having experienced all he wanted of Gerhardt's arrest techniques.

Examining Blagg's Browning shotgun, with its long magazine extension still in place, Mercer turned to the man and said, "You're in trouble, Charlie."

Blagg glanced over at the pile of ducks he had been carrying and thought of the huge pile of birds still remaining in the field. He then returned his attention to Mercer. There was no denying the warden's statement—he was definitely in trouble.

It took Gerhardt a few minutes to fish around in the canal and find Bates' shotgun—another extension-equipped Browning—then the wardens led the two poachers to the patrol car. An hour later, Bates and Blagg were behind bars in Oroville.

The driver who had dropped off the two shooters got away. Mercer found out later than it had been Donald Short, another habitual violator—an extremely lucky one.

Due to his disappointing experiences with the local courts, Mercer filed charges against the two market hunters through the federal court in Sacramento. Both men entered not-guilty pleas, and after lengthy court battles, both were convicted. The federal magistrate who presided over the proceedings saw no humor in the fact that both men had strings of past convictions for game-law violations, so, when it came time for sentencing, he socked each of them with a six-month term in the federal penitentiary and a five hundred dollar fine. Mercer was delighted.

During the trial, an outlaw brother-in-law of Charlie Blagg, who testified in Charlie's behalf, was caught perjuring himself. A few weeks later, the man was tried and convicted of perjury and soon joined Charlie and Lester in federal prison. Mercer was again delighted.

But the real payoff on this case came later, while Charlie Blagg and Lester Bates were cooling their heels in prison. Apparently Donald Short had always admired Charlie Blagg's wife, and while Charlie was tucked away in jail, Short started seeing her. Soon this affair became town gossip and it wasn't long before Charlie's brother, Edward Blagg, got wind of it.

Edward Blagg was enraged. Donald Short had been a friend of the Blaggs for years, and Edward couldn't imagine the man betraying Charlie like that. Edward stewed about this for several days, then made a decision. The Blaggs would have their revenge.

*　　　*　　　*

In the late spring of 1944, while Charlie Blagg and Lester Bates were still in prison, Mercer was surprised to get a phone call from Edward Blagg.

"I'm going to talk to you, Mercer, and I hope you'll hold my confidence," said Blagg.

"I'm listening," replied Mercer.

"If you let this out, my life won't be worth a nickel," Blagg continued, "but I've checked up on you and I know you won't talk."

"That's right," said Mercer. "What do you have to say?"

Blagg went on to tell Mercer about how Donald Short had moved in with his brother Charlie's wife and was living with her while Charlie was in prison. Mercer could feel the hatred in the man's words.

"I'm fed up with Don Short and all this market hunting stuff," Blagg continued bitterly. "I've decided to help you catch every damned market hunter I can."

Mercer was all ears.

"I'll be right around those people," said Blagg, "and I'll be able to tell you who has ducks and where they're keeping 'em—and when they're taking 'em to the city. I'll be able to tell you where they're goin', what they're drivin', and maybe the license number. When I call you, I'll identify myself as Sour-Wine—and I'll need your word that you'll keep this a total secret between you and me."

Mercer gave his word, but he was very skeptical that anything would come of it. After all, it was several months to waterfowl season, and Edward Blagg could do a lot of cooling off in that amount of time. Mercer was nearly certain that he would never hear from Sour-Wine. But he was wrong.

*   *   *

"Hello, Mercer? This is Sour-Wine," said the caller.

"Hello, Sour-Wine," Mercer replied.

It was now early November, and the first of the big northern flocks of ducks were arriving in the valley.

"Don Short shot up the ducks last night," said Sour-Wine, "and he has about two hundred of 'em. He and another guy will be taking 'em to Sacramento this evening. They'll be leaving in about a half hour from Gridley."

Sour-Wine then went on to describe the car—make, color, and license number.

"I appreciate it, Sour-Wine," replied Mercer. "I'll get right on it."

The information had a ring of truth to it, and Mercer

acted immediately. He was too far out of position to go personally, but he made some hurried calls and finally got through to U.S. Fish and Wildlife Agent Charles 'Chop' Fairchild in Sacramento. Fairchild took the information and agreed to watch for the vehicle on Highway 99, north of town.

Several hours later, Fairchild called back.

"You called it just right, Mercer. It was just like you said," reported Fairchild, sounding well pleased.

Donald Short and his friend had arrived right on schedule, and Fairchild and another agent had pulled them over and found more than two hundred ducks in the trunk. The two violators were now in jail in Sacramento.

"Scratch one up for Sour-Wine," thought Mercer.

A Bad Night for Snake

Night had come to the north valley, and a car containing three dark figures sped southward through the darkness. It traveled the River Road, along the west bank of the Sacramento River, through some of the finest waterfowl country in the world. Hidden in the trunk of the vehicle were several hundred illegally taken ducks, victims of a drag the night before. The birds were now on their way to be sold in San Francisco.

In the front seat, Snake McVey was worried. He peered back through the rear window, his odd serpentlike eyes squinting at the headlights of a sedan that had pulled onto the road behind them. He hadn't liked the looks of the car when they'd passed it a mile back, parked on the roadside south of Princeton, and now it was gaining on them at an alarming rate.

"What do you think, Snake?" asked Reggie Straight, who was doing the driving and nervously watching the rapidly approaching headlights in his rearview mirror.

"I think we've got trouble," replied Snake, and just then, a bright red light appeared over the headlights of the approaching sedan, confirming Snake's suspicions.

"Wardens!" shouted Snake.

Reggie cursed loudly and jammed the accelerator to the floor as the loud wail of a siren engulfed them. Their car shot ahead, but still the sedan gained on them. It was soon right on their tail.

"Hang on," said Reggie, as he wrenched hard on the wheel, throwing their car into a barely controlled, high-speed slide around a corner onto a side road. Accelerating out of the turn and barely missing a telephone pole, he glanced into his mirror and cursed again to find the pursuing sedan still glued to his rear bumper.

Snake, hanging on with both hands, searched his brain frantically for a way out of their predicament, acutely aware of the prison sentence they would face if caught with a trunkful of ducks. In the back seat, the third outlaw—who had come along on the promise of a wild night in the city—had wedged himself into a corner by the door, prepared to bolt from the vehicle at his first opportunity.

Reggie clung to the wheel with a death grip as he accelerated to top speed. It took all his concentration to keep the heavy vehicle on the rough, potholed surface of the roadway as the car hurtled through the night. But, behind him, the patrol car kept pace with apparent ease, red light blazing, siren screaming. Then the road made a sharp bend. Reggie braked hard, but wasn't able to make the turn. The car skidded off the road into a prune orchard, mowing down a row of young trees, but somehow remaining on its wheels. Reggie recovered quickly, accelerating again, steering straight through the middle of the orchard. Since he couldn't shake the pursuing sedan on the paved roads, he was determined now to lose it by going cross-country.

Despite the soft dirt, it was fairly easy going between the rows of trees, and both vehicles soon accelerated to a dangerous speed. But the far side of the orchard was fast approaching. Reggie saw the fence coming and aimed for a spot between two posts. The three strands of heavy barbed wire popped like old guitar strings as the car burst through the fence into a large expanse of rugged pasture. Reggie struck the first large bump with a jolt that nearly sent him and his passengers through the roof. Then it was one crashing impact after another, as the vehicles bounced and reeled across the moonlit pasture, sending livestock scattering in all directions.

When they came to a dirt road, Reggie steered onto it, thankful for some relief from the punishment they had been enduring. But the relief was short-lived, for a heavy wooden gate loomed across their path. Seeing no better options, Reggie gritted his teeth and aimed for the gate. He was accelerating when he struck it, dead center, sending shattered boards flying.

A farmer in a nearby farmhouse awoke to the frightful wail of a siren in his back pasture and the splintering crash of a vehicle demolishing his gate. Jumping from bed and running to a window, he was just in time to see the poachers' car—one headlight now missing and the patrol car hot on its tail—come careening around his barn and roar through his backyard and down his driveway toward the highway. He stood there, bewildered, squinting into the darkness, until the din of the siren and straining engines grew faint in the distance. Then, turning wearily, he walked over and climbed back into bed.

The chase had now led back to the River Road, with the two swift-moving vehicles rapidly approaching the town of Colusa. In the speeding patrol car, Warden Sabertooth Mercer was enjoying himself. It looked like another tip from his valued informant, Sour-Wine, was in the process of paying off, plus he was enjoying what so far was turning out to be a dandy chase. He was impressed with Warden Taylor London's masterful handling of the souped-up Ford patrol vehicle. He himself was a good high-speed driver, but he had to admit that London was better.

London took advantage of a straight stretch of highway to attempt to pass the poachers' vehicle, intent on crowding it off the road. But as the patrol car was creeping up the left side of the fleeing vehicle, Reggie swerved left, striking the patrol car a glancing blow, nearly sending it into a ditch. London recovered nicely, swearing softly under his breath, while Mercer sat unmoved. But, in the back seat, a new assistant warden was wishing desperately that he had chosen a different line of work.

London tried again to pass and was again nearly driven into the ditch. Then Mercer, who had decided that this business had gone far enough, removed the sawed-off shotgun from its rack. Directing the short, ugly barrel out the side window, he jacked a shell into the chamber. Then as London started again up the left side of the poachers' vehicle—and just as Reggie was preparing to swerve left again—Mercer fired a shot over the top of the vehicle.

While the deadly cluster of lead pellets passed at least two feet above Reggie's head, the muzzle-blast of the shotgun struck him like a punch. The result was instantaneous: Reggie hit the brakes, sending the sedan into a broadside skid, while London maneuvered desperately to avoid a collision. Remarkably, the poachers' car remained upright and both vehicles came to screeching halts, mere inches apart.

Reggie's car had no sooner stopped, when the doors flew open and all three poachers bolted for the moonlit orchards on either side of the road. Reggie went left, while Snake and the third man sprinted to the right.

But Mercer and London had anticipated a foot chase and had immediately sprung from the patrol car in close pursuit. London went after Reggie, while Mercer zeroed in on Snake and the third poacher. Mercer yelled for the assistant warden to follow, but the new man, shaken from the harrowing vehicle chase, was hesitant to respond.

Mercer could just make out the dark forms of the two fleeing men ahead in the moonlight. Glancing back, he found that he was alone, and a wave of anger swept over him. Where was the new man?

Then the dark forms ahead of him separated, forcing him to choose between them. He felt bitter at the prospect of one of the poachers escaping, but it couldn't be helped. He silently cursed the assistant warden as he raced along, gaining steadily on his quarry.

Snake McVey was now in a panic. When he and the other poacher had separated, he had hoped desperately that the pursuing warden would be drawn after the other man. But it hadn't happened that way. Now he could hear the threatening footfalls of the determined officer only a few yards behind him. Adrenaline and fear drove him onward, but that same fear was fast eroding his strength. He felt himself growing weaker each second.

Behind him, Mercer sensed that the time was right. Lowering his head, he drove forward with a burst of speed, knees pounding like pistons. Snake attempted to dodge the charge, but was too late. Mercer's tackle caught him low from behind, slamming him hard to the ground, face first, his nose plowing a furrow in the dirt. Then, after a brief tussle, Mercer muscled the struggling violator into submission and it was all over.

"Good evenin', Snake," said Mercer, recognizing his catch, but Snake McVey was in no condition to reply.

Back at the road, Reggie Straight waited sullenly in handcuffs while Taylor London worked at unloading several hundred nicely plucked ducks from the trunk of the captured vehicle. The new assistant warden stood uneasily nearby, nervously watching Mercer's approach with Snake, agonizing in his shame at having lost his nerve. When Mercer passed, he shot the new man a glance that nearly withered him in his shoes. Whether the man would ever again assist in warden's work was unknown, but it was absolutely certain that he would *never* again work with Mercer.

An hour later, Reggie Straight and Snake McVey—two of the worst market hunters in the state—were locked up in the Colusa County Jail.

*   *   *

Snake McVey was getting to know the Colusa County Jail pretty well, since it had been only a month earlier that he had spent a night there on another market-hunting arrest. However, a local jury—several members of which were poachers themselves—had found him not guilty of those charges, and he had immediately resumed his illegal market-hunting activities.

But Snake hadn't gotten away scot-free on that occasion. He had an uncle who was a hard-boiled, tough old game warden captain by the name of Stonewall Jackson Carpenter. Carpenter was a good man and rather sensitive about his market-hunting nephew, and he happened to be present at the Colusa Justice Court when Snake was acquitted by the crooked jury. He was also present on the courthouse steps, within earshot, when Snake did some crowing about his illegal activities and the inability of the wardens to make a case stick against him. Captain Stonewall Jackson Carpenter found these words particularly offensive and walking up behind his obnoxious nephew, he silenced the man with a sharp blow from his lead-cored leather sap. He then walked calmly away, leaving Snake McVey, out cold, stretched out in front of the courthouse like a dead carp.

Mercer and London had no intentions of entrusting Snake and Reggie again to some local jury. Instead, the wardens filed charges against them through federal court in Sacramento, and the two poachers soon found themselves before 'the hangin' judge.' The federal magistrate lived up to the wardens' best expectations by promptly sentencing Snake and Reggie to a three-month stay in the federal penitentiary.

A Raw Deal

Mercer moved quickly to cover the rear exit of the little house as Warden Roswell Tinnin pounded on the front door.

"State game wardens!" thundered Tinnin. "Open up, we have a search warrant."

From inside came the sound of muffled voices and the scrape of a chair on a wooden floor. Then footsteps, followed by the rattle of a latch and the creaking of old hinges.

Mercer could just barely hear the conversation as Tinnin explained the purpose of his visit to some male occupant of the house. Tinnin, the warden assigned to Yuba County, had received a report that someone at this residence in the tiny community of Arboga had killed a swan early that morning, and he and Mercer were there to investigate.

More footsteps and Tinnin's voice growing louder indicated to Mercer that the warden was now inside the dwelling. Mercer waited, as per their plan, for Tinnin to let him in through the back door.

"This is no big deal, but swans are protected birds and . . . ." Suddenly, Tinnin stopped cold in mid-sentence. Mercer leaned closer to the door, listening hard.

Then Tinnin began again, haltingly, "They're protected birds and ... uh ... you can't ... er ... Just a minute."

Mercer was puzzled, for Tinnin was usually confident and in total control of any situation. Then the back door opened and there stood Tinnin, blushing uncomfortably, an odd look on his face.

"What's the problem?" asked Mercer, as he stepped into the room.

A grim-faced man stood near a table where his two grown sons sat glowering at the wardens. Mercer turned questioningly to Tinnin, then froze as he saw the woman of the house. A handsome woman in her mid-thirties, she was busy at work in her kitchen, puttering unconcerned amid her pots and pans, apparently fixing dinner. It was a completely normal domestic scene, except for one thing—she was stark naked.

Mercer gawked for a moment in disbelief, then turned, red-faced, to the man of the house who stood scowling at him. "Have the lady put on some clothes," said Mercer.

"It's her house," replied the man. "She don't need no clothes."

Mercer turned to Tinnin who just shrugged his shoulders, a silly grin on his face. Then Mercer thought for a second. The man was right. There was no law requiring people to wear clothes in their own homes. With this settled in his mind, he returned his attention to the problem of the illegally taken swan.

"Sir, we know you've got a swan in here somewhere, so why not save yourself some trouble and give it to us now? Otherwise we'll have to search for it," said Mercer.

The man hesitated a few seconds, then turned to his wife. "Show 'em the swan, Flo."

The woman, who had made no attempt to cover up, strolled over and opened the oven door. With a pair of pot holders she removed a large, covered roasting pan and set it on top the stove.

Mercer tried first looking at the floor ... then the

ceiling ... then out the window. It didn't seem right to stare. Tinnin was having his own uncomfortable time of it, standing awkwardly, making a show of examining his fingernails.

"Here it is," they heard her say, and both turned to focus on a scene that would remain with them forever, permanently etched in their memories.

She stood casually, facing them, one hand on her hip, the other holding up the lid she had just removed from the roasting pan. The look on her face was one of bored indifference. A cloud of pungent-smelling steam was rising from the pan, which the wardens were vaguely aware contained some kind of large, baked bird.

Upon regaining his senses, Mercer wrinkled his nose in disgust at the unpleasant aroma of the swan. He would later describe it as smelling like "ten pounds of baked horse manure."

One of the two sons finally admitted to killing the swan, and Tinnin hurriedly scratched out a citation. The wardens then packed the half-baked bird into a grain sack, stole one last disbelieving glance at the unclad housewife, and hastened on their way.

Arboga residents paused to watch curiously as the Fish and Game car left town, traveling rather erratically, its driver so convulsed with mirth that he could barely keep it on the road.

A Long-Shot Pays Off

The buck stood frozen in the poacher's spotlight beam, confused and vulnerable. Its eyes were aglow with reflected light, shining as though powered by their own electricity. Its forked antlers, still in velvet, gleamed in the harsh light like burnished bronze.

Nearby, on the road across the meadow, an old flatbed truck was stopped, engine idling. The driver trained the spotlight on the deer, while another man leaned from the window, squinting down the barrel of a battered rifle. The rifle bucked as the shot rang out, sounding incredibly loud in the still, summer night. The stricken buck went instantly to its knees, then onto its side, where it lay gasping, legs flailing the air. Then it was still.

The driver cut lights and engine, and both men stepped out into the darkness, where they stood quietly for a time, just listening. They were not young men, but veterans of more than forty years of game poaching, and they knew what precautions to take. When satisfied they were alone, they hurriedly gathered some gear from the truck and started across the meadow toward the deer.

But they stopped short after only a few yards.

Standing dead still, they listened again and peered up Humbug Road to the east. Though they could see nothing, there was definitely the sound of an engine. A car was approaching.

"Let's get out of here," said one of them, and they turned quickly and sprinted back to their car. Seconds later, they were racing down the hill, trailing clouds of fine dust that boiled up behind them to hang suspended in the still air.

*   *   *

Mercer, at his camp, had just sat down to a late dinner when the rifle shot brought him back to his feet.

"That was close," he thought, as he stood listening for another shot, which never came. He set his plate down on a stump, grabbed his hat, and headed for his patrol car.

His camp, in the tiny meadow known as Cuddyback Flat, was hidden back among the pines in the mountains east of Chico. From camp it was a mere 150 yards down to the old stage route known as Humbug Road. This old track snaked its way for miles up the timbered ridges, past Cuddyback Flat and Butte Creek House, and on through some of the finest deer country in the western Sierras.

Only seconds after leaving camp, Mercer pulled onto Humbug Road and started down the hill toward Stirling City, a logging community twelve miles to the south. He traveled at a moderate speed, without headlights, his sharp nighthawk eyes guiding him over the rutted surface.

He wasn't pleased to be using his vehicle to blindly chase a poacher's shot, for at best, the odds were well against him. Most probably the poachers would hear him coming in time to get away. But he *had* to use the patrol car, for it was simply too far to walk in a reasonable amount of time.

It was a frustrating thing, for there was no good way to handle these situations. Had he been between the poachers and town, he might have gambled and waited on the road for them to come to him, but under the circumstances, waiting tonight would be a poor bet. He could only hope for some luck. There was always the chance that the shot had been a miss and he could surprise the poachers still in their car, working a spotlight.

He continued on through the dim moonlight, a tight grip on the wheel. It was rough going, but he was able to dodge the worst of the bumps and potholes, most of which he knew by heart. Then he rounded a bend and encountered a curtain of dust suspended over the roadway.

"This must have been the spot," he thought, as he made a mental note, picking landmarks that would guide him back. He doubted that the poachers would have had time enough to load the deer—assuming, of course, that there even *was* a deer.

He accelerated now, certain that the suspects were on the road ahead of him. Judging from the amount of dust, he suspected they had heard him coming and were traveling pretty fast. The patrol car bucked and reeled on the rugged old road, which was now obscured by dust as well as darkness. Mercer could see well enough to get by without his headlights, but it required his complete concentration.

Approaching the remote three-way intersection known as Chaparral Junction. Mercer was surprised to see the dust trail lead to the right onto Bull Hill Road. He had expected the suspects to continue down the hill toward Stirling City, but instead they had doubled back. He knew he was gaining on them, for the dust trail was becoming more dense and he was having more trouble seeing the road.

A minute or two later, he caught a glimpse of taillights before they disappeared around a bend. The poachers had slowed considerably, apparently thinking they were safe, and Mercer closed rapidly on them. When less than five car lengths separated the two vehicles, the dust was so thick that Mercer could not see to approach closer. He backed off on the accelerator and held his position, his eyes locked on the twin taillights glowing dimly ahead through the billowing dust. Finally, brake lights flashed and the suspects turned left down a narrow track that wound through the timber to a mining claim on the bank of Bull Creek. As they pulled to a stop, Mercer was right on their tail and caught a glimpse of a tent and a cluttered camp in the glare of their headlights.

The first indication the poachers had of Mercer's presence came when their lights went off and Mercer's flashed on. They turned quickly to peer back into the two bright orbs behind them, then glanced at one another in distress.

"If that's Mercer, we've had it," said the driver. He then muttered a foul oath as he and his companion stepped down from the cab of the truck.

As Mercer approached the two men, he was well aware that his task would not be an easy one. He knew the men had been up to no good, but he had very little on which to build a case. He didn't even know for sure if they'd killed anything. True, the situation was a real long-shot, but it was worth a try. He prepared himself mentally, for any chance for success would depend on skillful handling and questioning of the suspects ... but these were things at which Mercer happened to be very good.

"State game warden," announced Mercer. "I'll need to see some identification from you men."

"What's this all about?" asked one of the men, fumbling for his wallet and squinting against the headlights at Mercer.

"You know very well what this is about," Mercer replied. "Where's the rifle?"

"What rifle?" the man asked.

Mercer then took a couple of steps closer and replied

as though somewhat irritated, "Hey, I'm not here to play games with you guys. You're in some trouble . . . and if you don't cooperate you're going to be in some worse trouble. Now, where's the rifle?"

The man pointed meekly at the truck.

Shining his flashlight into the cab, Mercer spotted not only the old rifle, but a bundle of other implements on the floor, the tools of serious deer poachers. There were several cotton meat sacks, blood-stained from previous use; there was a spotlight wired into a car battery; and there was a meat saw, a cleaver, and several sharp knives.

"You guys meant business," said Mercer, as he gathered up the items and arranged them on the meat sacks which he had placed on the hood of the suspects' truck. "What's going to happen?" one of them asked.

Mercer just pointed to the passenger door of the patrol car and said "Climb in—first we have to go back and pick up the deer."

Dreading the likely "What deer?" reply, Mercer was amazed to see the two men march obediently to the patrol car and climb in. He wasted no time taking his seat at the wheel.

During the ride back to the spot on Humbug Road, Mercer kept the men engrossed in conversation— anything to keep them from serious consideration of their position. It was a delicate situation. Mercer could hardly believe they were going along with him, but things could change at any second. And if the suspects simply chose to deny knowledge of a deer, he would be left with nothing. Mercer slowed the patrol car as he approached the spot where he had first encountered the dust. It was the critical moment. He made a show of leaning forward, peering through the windshield as though searching for some special landmark.

"Let's see now, where is it?" he muttered, as though to himself.

"Up a ways," said one of the men, and Mercer drove on.

"Here," said the same man, and Mercer pulled over, breathing an inward sigh of relief.

The buck was there where it had fallen, still warm to the touch. Mercer made short work of field dressing the animal, and with the help of the two suspects, he soon had it loaded into the trunk of his patrol car. Back at their camp, the two poachers signed their citations and watched miserably as Mercer drove off with the deer, their rifle, and their poaching gear—all of which was later confiscated by a Butte County judge.

Mercer made a leisurely drive back to Cuddyback Flat where he found things just as he'd left them. He hung the deer from a beam nailed between two trees, then picked up his plate and resumed his meal.

A Taste of Fear

It began as a routine night patrol in the mountains of Butte County, a week before deer season in the fall of 1950. Warden Gene Mercer left his mountain camp at Cuddyback Flat shortly before dark and headed his patrol car down the crooked old Humbug Road. As he drove along, he fiddled with the knobs on his newly installed radio receiver, a device which later that night would save his life. It wasn't even a two-way radio. You couldn't talk to anyone . . . only listen. But it was a step in the right direction. Fish and Game was considering equipping its wardens with two-way radios, and to determine the range of reception in the mountains, the department installed radio receivers, tuned to the Highway Patrol's frequency, in the patrol vehicles of a few of the best wardens. These men were to record their location and the time of day anytime they heard radio transmissions. Mercer had been dutifully logging these transmissions for nearly a month.

At the remote three-way intersection known as Chaparral Junction, Mercer took the left fork toward Stirling City, then backed off the road into a small clearing he had hacked out of the forest. From there, nearly hidden, he could watch the junction and be in position to pounce on a spotlighter, should one happen by.

After covering the exposed front of his patrol car with a camouflage parachute, he crawled up onto the hood, leaned back against the windshield, and settled down to wait. Overhead, high clouds were closing in, obscuring an already unfriendly sky, and when darkness fell, it brought with it the threat of rain.

The hours passed slowly, with only a car or two going by shortly after dark, just travelers passing through. After that, all was quiet . . . except for the wind. It wasn't a strong wind, just enough to set the pines rustling, but it blew with a cold edge that bore the promise of an early winter. Mercer shivered and burrowed deeper into his heavy jacket.

It was after midnight when he heard the shot, a dull report off to the east. Nearly lost in the wind, it could easily have been missed, but it brought Mercer instantly alert, peering off through the forest, judging distance and direction.

"That couldn't have been too far from my camp," he thought, as he vaulted down from the hood of his car and began gathering up the parachute. Seconds later, he had started the car and was creeping along, without lights, to take up a position to stop anything coming down Humbug Road.

After only a ten-minute wait, he heard the faint grind of an engine and caught the first flash of approaching headlights. His pulse quickened as he felt the familiar butterfly-flutter in his stomach, experiencing feelings not unlike those of a sprinter waiting for the gun. He took a deep breath and steeled himself for the impending encounter . . . it took nerve to stand alone in the night and face armed men.

Then they were upon him. The approaching sedan wheeled into sight around the curve and Mercer met it head-on, headlights blazing, his red spotlight bathing the scene in an eerie pink glow. The driver of the sedan had no choice but to jam on the brakes, and the two vehicles came to rest less than ten feet apart. Mercer was out immediately, flashlight in hand, striding forward. He slipped quickly between the two cars and approached the driver of the sedan.

"State game warden, turn off your engine," shouted Mercer, shining his flashlight inside the vehicle.

The driver and two other men sat staring out at him from the front seat, still in shock from the suddenness of the stop. Shifting his beam to the back seat, Mercer spotted a forked-horn buck laid out on a piece of blood-stained canvas, its eyes still clear and shining.

Returning his attention to the driver, Mercer recognized the man.

"Harter ... not you again," he said. "Don't you ever learn?"

Dan Harter, a local logger and a habitual poacher, switched off the ignition and peered grimly out at Mercer. It had been only a month since Mercer had last caught him spotlighting, and the experience had proven costly. Now he was about to go through it all again.

Mercer scrutinized the three suspects, noting their glassy eyes and flushed faces, signs that they'd been drinking ... and subtle warnings to Mercer. An almost empty whiskey bottle lay on the floor near some spent cartridge cases, and a lever-action .30-30 rifle was resting, butt down, against the seat between the two passengers.

"I'll need some identification from you men," said Mercer, still standing at the driver's window with his light directed inside. But there was no move by any of the men to comply.

"All right, get out of the car," said Mercer in a stern voice, stepping closer to open the driver's door.

Harter reluctantly stepped out, but the others stayed where they were, following Mercer's every move with hostile eyes. Mercer directed Harter to stand in the headlights between the two cars, then hurried to the other side of the car and opened the passenger door.

"Get out," he said. "I'm not going to tell you again

—and leave the rifle where it is."

The man closest to the door, a gaunt, sinister-looking individual by the name of Conley, stepped out and Mercer led him to the front of the car with Harter. This left a hard-looking individual by the name of Barth still in the car.

Morris Barth was a dangerous man . . . or so some people believed. Not only was he a bully with an obvious mean streak, but the other loggers with whom he worked felt that he wasn't quite right in the head. But he could fell trees with unusual skill, a talent that ensured him permanent employment with Diamond Match Company. He required very little out of life, content to fell timber, raise hell at the Bambi Inn Saloon . . . and poach deer.

Up to this point, Barth had been lucky in his poaching activities, somehow evading arrest in a part of the country patrolled by a particularly tough, hardworking warden. But his luck had run out, and now, face-to-face with that warden, and caught red-handed with a deer, his reaction was that of an animal brought to bay. When he came out of the vehicle, he came out in a hurry, and Mercer was alarmed to see him dragging the rifle out with him.

"Hold it," yelled Mercer, crouching and reaching to his belt for his pistol. With a sinking feeling, he realized that the weapon wasn't there.

Never one to carry a gun on routine patrol, Mercer packed his service pistol only when he anticipated a dangerous situation. True enough, a head-on stop of poachers at night was plenty dangerous, but this time he had simply forgotten to stick the weapon into his belt. Now he was in trouble, and his pistol—which was only a few feet away on the front seat of his patrol car—might as well have been on the moon.

Doing the next best thing, he rushed forward, trying to get to the rifle before Barth could bring it to bear, but he was too late. He froze when Barth whirled to face him, holding the weapon threateningly.

"Hey, mister, you don't want that kind of trouble," said Mercer. "Put the gun down."

He took a step toward Barth and held out his hand as though to take the weapon. Barth took a quick step back, jacked a live round into the chamber and lowered the barrel directly at Mercer's stomach.

"Hold it right there, Mr. Game Warden," said Barth menacingly, his speech slightly slurred by the whiskey. He glared at Mercer with the wild, unblinking eyes of one on the brink of insanity, and Mercer felt the hackles rise on the back of his neck.

"Shoot him, Barth," cried Conley. "We can't afford no fine."

"What do you say to that, Mr. Game Warden?" asked Barth, breaking into a horrible grin, which, in the glare of the headlights, revealed a mouthful of rotten teeth. He was beginning to enjoy himself, holding the most troublesome of the local game wardens at gunpoint, totally at his mercy.

"What about his car?" asked Harter nervously. Harter was the most rational of the three men, yet quite capable of murder.

"We can drive it off somewhere and hide it," answered Barth. "They won't find him *or* the car for days."

This apparently satisfied Harter, and the matter seemed to be settled.

Garth gestured with the rifle barrel toward the brush alongside the road and said, "Start walkin', Mercer."

Mercer had first experienced anger as the three men coldly discussed whether or not he should live or die, but now he felt a new emotion—a choking, bitter thing that welled up in his throat like bile. And mingled with his fear was a deep regret as he thought of his wife and daughter, wishing he had spent more time with them.

But he forced his fear aside, setting his mind to work, carefully evaluating his options, judging his chances. He had talked his way out of some bad spots over the years, but nothing like this. It would take more than talking to get him through this one.

"I said, start walking," Barth repeated, bringing the rifle up to his shoulder, pointing it now at Mercer's head.

But Mercer stood his ground and looked Barth square in the eyes.

"I'm not going anywhere," he said, speaking urgently, ". . . and you'd better think about what you're doing. If you go through with this, you'll be lookin' over your shoulder for the rest of your life . . . which won't be long when the other wardens find out."

"It's too late, Mercer, you're a dead man," said Barth with cruel satisfaction.

Mercer knew he didn't have a chance. He knew he was going to die, and he accepted the fact calmly, but he refused to stand and be slaughtered like an animal. Instead, he prepared himself to attack, to inflict as much damage as he could on the three men before he lost consciousness. His eyes narrowed as he glared at Morris Barth, hating the man, longing to get his fingers on that stubbled throat. He gathered his strength and was about to lunge for Barth when suddenly the radio receiver in the patrol car came alive with a burst of static and garbled voices.

"What was that?" asked Barth, thoroughly startled, looking over at the patrol car.

"That's my radio," answered Mercer. "You guys are gonna be in jail by morning."

"What do you mean?" asked Barth, again peering down the rifle barrel at Mercer.

"I told 'em I was makin' a stop . . . they're on their way," Mercer replied.

Conley stepped forward and cried, "Don't listen to him, Barth, he's bluffing! Kill him and let's get out of here."

But Harter was having second thoughts and said, "Hey wait a minute, Barth, this is gettin' too risky . . . you can count me out. I don't want anything to do with this." He walked off a short distance, shaking his head.

Mercer set his mind to pursuing this shred of hope.

"Think of the chance you're takin', Barth," he said. "Sooner or later Harter will talk. Just think about it."

Barth brought the rifle down from his shoulder, but still kept the muzzle trained on Mercer.

"Don't let him talk you out of it, Barth," Conley implored. "He's just . . ."

"Shut up, Conley," interrupted Barth. "Just shut your mouth!"

The situation was having a sobering effect on Barth. Mercer could almost *see* the man's head clearing as he kept glancing nervously down the road toward Stirling City, as though at any second another green patrol car would appear.

"Lay the gun down, Barth," coaxed Mercer in a low voice. "You can walk away from this with just a citation. You don't want to go to prison."

"He's right, Barth," said Harter. "This has gone far enough."

Barth looked down at the rifle in his hands then back at Mercer.

"Lay it down, Barth," said Mercer gently.

Barth let out a long sigh and gave his head a quick shake, as though recovering from a punch. He then turned slowly and placed the rifle on the hood of Mercer's car. Mercer stepped forward and picked it up.

*   *   *

It was just breaking daylight when the rain came, and Mercer was still awake in his tent at Cuddyback Flat. He lay on his back on his cot, with his fingers laced behind his head, staring up at the ceiling. He was contemplating things he had long taken for granted. He marveled at the delightful patter of raindrops on canvas, and the wonderful, pungent aroma of damp earth. He thought it strange he had never noticed these things before.

It was great being in the mountains at dawn on a rainy morning, and it was great being a game warden . . . but most of all, it was *great* being alive.

A Threat from an Old Enemy

Hard-working wardens, in the course of their duties, are bound to step on a few toes now and then. It simply goes with the job. Nobody likes to receive a citation, and while most people simply shrug off the experience as being their own fault, some blame the warden. A few go so far as to develop a genuine hatred for the warden, and if they happen to be vindictive, the warden may find himself with dangerous enemies. Mercer made his share of enemies over the years, and once, in the spring of 1951, an encounter with an old enemy led to an important court decision.

There was a rendering plant, known as the tallow works, located beside Robinson Creek, halfway between Chico and Oroville, and one morning, the owner of the plant called Mercer to report a violation. Some boys in their mid- to late teens were walking the creek and illegally shooting ducks, pheasants, and anything else they could get in their sights. Mercer left for the area immediately.

Upon arriving at the tallow works, Mercer had no trouble spotting the four boys. Armed with shotguns and .22 rifles, they were hunting along the creek no more than a third of a mile to the west. As Mercer watched through his binoculars, one of the boys shot an egret that was standing on a small island in the creek. The graceful, snowy white bird collapsed in the mud and died, and its killer made no attempt whatsoever to retrieve it.

Mercer was tight-jawed as he started for his patrol car to go after the destructive youths, but he stopped when he saw a car pull off the highway and drive over to them. The boys immediately loaded a number of what appeared to be ducks and pheasants into the trunk of the vehicle, which then turned around and started back toward the main road. Mercer was ready for it and made a head-on stop.

The driver, an arrogant young man in his early twenties, was troublesome from the start.

"What are you stopping me for?" he demanded. "I haven't done anything!"

"I'll need to see your driver's license," said Mercer, standing at the driver's door, "and I'll need to see the birds you've got in the trunk."

The youth fumbled through his wallet in apparent outrage, jerked out his driver's license, and thrust it at Mercer. Mercer regarded the name on the license, William Franklin Marizanni, then looked up to study the young man with interest.

"Yes," Mercer thought, "there definitely is a resemblance."

"You're Frank's boy, aren't you," said Mercer. It was more of a statement than a question.

"That's right," the young man answered, "and he's not going to be happy about this."

It had been over twenty years since Mercer had seen Frank Marizanni, a wealthy bootlegger and game poacher in the Portola area of Plumas County. Mercer had tangled with him on several occasions, and Marizanni had developed an intense hatred for Mercer. Mercer had heard that Marizanni had sold out in Portola and moved to the valley to run a gravel plant south of Chico. Mercer had known then that sooner or later he and Marizanni would cross paths again.

After considerable protest, Marizanni's obnoxious son finally opened the trunk, from which Mercer pulled out a variety of out-of-season game birds. Mercer then issued young Marizanni a citation and sent him on his way. The youth then made a beeline for his father's gravel pits. Mercer loaded the seized birds into his car and headed for the creek to retrieve the dead egret. He could still see the four youths off in the distance.

Robinson Creek, in that area, was a foul-smelling, greasy mess, due to the nasty stuff pumped into it from the tallow works. But Mercer hesitated only briefly, then waded in, his mouth set in a grimace and his nose wrinkled in disgust. Reaching the island, he picked up the once-beautiful white bird, now soiled and lifeless, and experienced a small pain in his heart over such senseless waste.

When he turned and started back for the bank, he was surprised to see the owner of the land, Abe Bateman, waiting for him. The man was grinning widely at the sight of Mercer slogging along waist-deep in the foul water.

"You're a brave man, Mercer," chided Bateman, who backed up a step or two as Mercer approached, realizing that the warden had acquired the same unpleasant aroma as that of the polluted creek.

Mercer grumbled a suitable return, then looked a-round at the sound of an approaching vehicle. A pickup truck had arrived on the opposite side of the creek, and two men got out. The driver was George Dutra, a stout, humorless man who was Marizanni's foreman at the gravel operation. During the preceding ten years, Mercer had arrested most of the male members of Dutra's family, and Dutra didn't look too happy to see him. Dutra's passenger was Big Frank Marizanni himself.

"He hasn't changed much," thought Mercer as Marizanni stormed toward him, fuming, stopping only when he reached the water. The old outlaw was still a large, intimidating bully of a man, and at that moment his face was flushed red with anger.

"Mercer, you son of a bitch," he sputtered, "these boys were just havin' some fun. They weren't hurtin' nobody. I'm gonna get you, Mercer. If you were over here, I'd break your back!"

"Don't be threatening me, Frank," said Mercer. "It's against the law to threaten a federal deputy, and that's what I am."

"I don't care what you are, Mercer, you've hounded me enough. It may be a month or a year, but I'll get you for this," said Marizanni.

"And if Frank don't get you, I will," added Dutra, glaring at Mercer.

Mercer considered the belligerent men for a moment longer, then directed his attention to the back of the pickup. There were four boys in their mid-teens sitting there—probably more of Marizanni's kids—and Mercer recognized them as his illegal shooters. He could now see they were all juveniles, which meant he had waded after the egret for nothing—none of the local judges would prosecute juveniles on game charges. But his case against the oldest Marizanni boy was sound, and he had made a decision to go after Frank Marizanni and George Dutra for threatening him.

With no further reason to stay around and be berated by Marizanni, Mercer got into his car and left. But before going, he addressed the two men across the creek.

"I'll be seeing you men soon," he said, "... maybe sooner than you think."

*   *   *

A month later, Frank Marizanni and George Dutra found themselves before a federal magistrate in Sacramento, facing charges of threatening a federal officer (all state wardens were—and still are—federal deputies). Abe Bateman, the landowner who was with Mercer during the incident, was a reluctant, but highly effective, witness for the prosecution, and due largely to his testimony, Marizanni and Dutra were promptly convicted. Both were fined three hundred dollars and placed on three years probation. Mercer left the courtroom well satisfied. This case was an important one to Fish and Game, for it set a precedent as being the first case in which anyone was ever successfully prosecuted for threatening a game warden. Mercer had attempted it four months earlier, following his narrow escape from three half-drunk poachers who very nearly killed him, but the local judge was of the opinion that wardens were paid to take that kind of abuse. So, the three poachers were convicted of spotlighting a deer, but they escaped even a verbal reprimand for holding a state game warden at riflepoint and coming within a hairbreadth of murdering him in cold blood.

Gettin' Lucky

The call came at around midnight, waking the dozen or so game wardens curled up in sleeping bags scattered around the forest clearing. Some were now up, but most were still in their bags, propped up on one elbow, listening intently to the new two-way radio mounted in Mercer's patrol car.

"Could you repeat?" queried Warden Gene Mercer, a microphone pressed to his lips. "Understand you have spotlighters killing deer off Newville Road on the Flood Ranch?"

"That's affirmative," responded a feminine voice, nearly drowned out by static. "The caller thinks they've killed several deer and left without picking them up."

"Did he get their direction of travel?" asked Mercer.

"That's unknown, but the caller thinks they're still in the same general area," the dispatcher replied.

"Ten-four and thanks," said Mercer, signing off. He replaced the microphone in its metal clip on the dashboard.

The wardens were gathered for a two-day squad meeting in the mountains above Chico. They were camped in a small meadow next to their captain's newly purchased cabin at Philbrook Reservoir. They had spent the first day going over time reports and other state

business, then they'd barbequed steaks in the evening
and sat around the campfire telling 'war stories.' It was
unknown, as yet, what the captain had planned for the
following day, but the wardens had been eyeing, with
growing suspicion, the pile of building materials—
including paint brushes and several gallons of paint—
stacked on the front porch of the newly acquired cabin.

Mercer turned to Warden Jim Hiller, the Willows
warden, a close friend whom he greatly respected.

"I don't know, Saber," said Hiller, anticipating the
question. "That's a long way from here." It was true.
To get to the Flood Ranch, they would first have to twist
their way down forty miles of poor mountain road just
to get them out of the Sierras. Then there would come
a relatively straight twenty-five-mile stretch, west across
the Sacramento Valley to the foothills of the Coast Range.
From there, it would be an additional fifteen crooked
miles through the foothills. They were looking at several
hours of hard travel.

"We can only try," said Mercer. "Maybe we'll get lucky."

Hiller nodded in agreement, and the two wardens
turned to the captain who was standing sleepy-eyed
in his long johns in the doorway of his cabin.

"We've got a call, Captain, we're gonna have to go,"
said Mercer. Then he and Hiller hurried over and
gathered up their bedrolls and piled them into Mercer's
brand-new 1952 Ford patrol car.

"You drive," said Mercer. It was well known that Hiller
had been a race car driver and was highly skilled at
the wheel. Seconds later, Hiller had the patrol car in
gear and they were on their way, leaving the other
wardens and their disgruntled captain behind. Mercer
was on the radio again, notifying the dispatcher that
they were on their way.

Mercer, remembering the paint and building materials, turned to Hiller with a grin and said, "Sure hate
to miss out on tomorrow!"

"Yeah, me too," said Hiller with a chuckle, as he shifted
into high gear.

Neither warden got along well with the captain and avoided him whenever possible. Only a week earlier, they had been driving along together, patrolling the valley, when the captain called Hiller on the radio.

"Where are you, Hiller?" asked the captain.

"I'm up on Sheet Iron Mountain," fibbed Hiller, referring to a place some fifty miles away to the west.

Then the captain tried Mercer.

"How about you, Mercer, where are you?" asked the Captain.

Mercer took the mike from Hiller and answered, "I'm up at Bottle Hill Lookout," referring to a place some fifty miles to the east.

He and Hiller then looked at each other and grinned. But the humor of the moment was cut short when, to their horror, they spotted the captain coming down the road right at them. There was no time to turn off or hide or do anything but get caught. He had them dead to rights.

But when he got to them, he went right on by, with no sign of recognition whatsoever. He was apparently lost in thought, his mind elsewhere, and he never even saw them. When the two wardens had recovered enough to regain their sense of humor, they laughed until they were nearly unconscious.

The ride down from Philbrook that night was an experience Mercer would not soon forget. Hiller pushed the Ford to the limit, expertly dodging deer and skidding around the turns at maximum speed. Mercer hung on for all he was worth.

When they roared through Stirling City, they switched on red light and siren, waking most of the residents and setting every dog in town barking or howling. Paradise residents got more of the same, the patrol car blasting through town with red light and wailing siren.

Reaching the valley, Hiller *really* turned the new Ford loose, and they almost flew through the farm country. They slowed only a little to negotiate the steel bridge over the Sacramento River, and again to pass through the town of Orland. When they reached the foothills of the Coast Range, the road turned bad again and it was after 2:30 A.M. when they finally rolled into the driveway of the Flood Ranch.

Leo Flood explained that the shooting had occurred somewhere along the road between his place and his son's house, which was a couple of miles farther west up Newville Road. He had been on the phone with his son just a few minutes earlier, and his son had reported that no vehicles had been by—which indicated that the poachers were still somewhere between his son's place and his own.

"The deer are thicker than fleas out there . . . I'm sure they got some down," said Leo Flood.

After considering their options, the wardens decided to risk a drive through the area to the younger Flood's house to see what they could see. But the winding drive through the night-darkened foothills revealed nothing. They saw only the bright, reflective eyes of more than a dozen seemingly half-tame deer, and a number of sheep.

Yet, there was one thing that both wardens noticed. When they passed a freshly harvested barley field, a place where there should have been deer, they saw nothing— not even sheep. When their headlights flashed across expanses of the field it appeared to be empty. It was a long, narrow field with the road running along its north side and the willow-choked banks of Little Stony Creek on the other. Opposite the field, a road cut to the right off Newville Road, winding to the north, up an oak-studded hillside. Hiller said it led to a small cemetery.

Lyle Flood was waiting in his driveway when the wardens arrived. He was excited. He had just been on the hill behind his house, and he had seen what appeared to be flashlights in the barley field across from the cemetery road, back toward his dad's house. The flashlights had disappeared when the patrol car came through.

Following a short conversation with Lyle Flood, the wardens made their way over a back road—little more than a cattle trail—that took them to the rear of the old cemetery. They parked the patrol car there and continued on foot, picking their way carefully down the cemetery road. It was hard to see, for while the sky was clear, the moon had long since slipped behind the mountains, and only starlight saved the night from total darkness. When the wardens reached the Newville Road, across from the barley field, they burrowed into some tall grass and settled down to wait.

The time passed slowly, the wardens peering into the night, straining eyes and ears for signs of the poachers, but there was nothing. And yet something wasn't right—it was just too quiet.

"Do you feel it, Saber?" asked Hiller in a whisper.

"Yeah, I feel it," answered Mercer. "They're out there somewhere."

But there was nothing to do but wait ... and their waiting, in the frigid predawn hours after being up all night, was slow torture.

Then there was a faint glow to the east, which slowly grew until the darkness began to fade. In the first gray light of dawn, the wardens could see the long, straw-stubbled field of harvested barley, which, strangely enough, had a massive oak tree growing in the middle of it. Mercer wondered why the farmers had allowed such an obstacle to remain, then decided that they had probably felt, as he did, that the tree was simply too magnificent to destroy.

Suddenly Mercer detected movement in the field, barely visible in the dim light. He tapped Hiller on the shoulder and pointed to a spot slightly left of the oak tree. Hiller nodded and trained his binoculars on the spot.

"There's somebody out there," whispered Hiller. "Looks like he's dragging something ... It's gotta be a deer."

Mercer borrowed the binoculars, scanned the area,

and promptly spotted two more man-shaped silhouettes
in the field. One was kneeling and appeared to be field
dressing a deer, while the other was standing and
keeping watch. The first suspect dragged his deer to
the base of the oak tree, then walked back the way he
had come. Soon, he produced a knife and began working
on yet another deer.

Keeping a close eye on the suspects, the wardens eased
their way across Newville Road and crept in behind a
low scrub oak at the edge of the barley field. From there,
they would have to cover more than two hundred feet
of open ground to reach the deer poachers. Speaking
in whispers, they made their plan. Since neither of them
was in uniform, they would simply walk out to the
suspects and hope that the men would think they were
something other than wardens.

Waiting until all three suspects were busily working
on deer, the wardens made their move. They stood up,
stepped over a low spot in the sheep fence, and started
across the field. They forced themselves to hold their
pace to a leisurely walk. Two of the suspects were still
together, kneeling in the barley stubble, intent on their
work, but the third was out a ways farther by himself.
It was the third man who looked up and spotted the
wardens before they had made it halfway to the oak
tree. He immediately stood up and called to the others.

Resisting the temptation to charge forward, the
wardens continued their unhurried pace, and Mercer
even managed to smile and wave at the suspects. The
puzzled suspects stood staring at the intruders,
regarding them with a mixture of apprehension and
hostility. But they didn't run, and the wardens were
able to walk right up on the two who were closest.

"Who are you?" one of the poachers demanded.

In answer, Mercer pulled his vest aside, revealing his
badge pinned to his flannel shirt.

"State game wardens, men," said Mercer. "Stay right
where you are."

One of the poachers just stared at the wardens in

disbelief, while the other looked around frantically, searching for some escape. But it was too late, the wardens were too close.

While it was too late for the first two suspects, the third man still had a chance. Mercer had hoped to get closer to him, but the man was now walking away, looking back over his shoulder. When Mercer started after him, he ran, heading for Stony Creek at a steady lope. Mercer was torn with the decision whether to go after the fleeing suspect, or stay and help Hiller with the first two. Glancing back at Hiller, he decided to stay, for one of the two men was acting as though he might try something, and Mercer had long ago learned the wisdom of the old 'bird in the hand' adage.

Hiller demanded identification from the two captured poachers, and they fumbled through their wallets and produced driver's licenses. Both were young men in their mid-twenties, ashen-faced, visibly shaking, their hands and lower arms covered with fresh blood.

Hiller studied the licenses. "You both still live in Chico?" he asked.

The suspects nodded to the affirmative.

Mercer took a moment to look around, and was amazed at what he saw. From where he stood he could see the carcasses of at least five deer lying in the barley stubble. Two had been dragged to the base of the oak tree, and three others were still lying where they had fallen to the poacher's bullets.

"Where are your guns?" Mercer asked, turning to face the two suspects.

But before either suspect could answer, Mercer caught sight of another man walking their way, coming from the west along Stony Creek. He was carrying a rifle and looking down into the willows along the creek. Mercer was certain he was another of the poachers, and it appeared that he was unaware, as yet, that anything was amiss.

Mercer quickly knelt down beside the deer the two men had been working on. He ordered the two men to do the same. He then lay down in the barley stubble, keeping the two men between him and the approaching suspect. Hiller turned his back on all of them and walked a short distance to one of the other deer and knelt down beside it.

As the gun-bearing suspect approached, Mercer was out of sight, and the man could see only three people in the field—the number he expected to see. Mercer had ordered the two suspects to resume their work on the deer beside them, and Hiller appeared to be working on another one. And so, in the dim light, nothing appeared threatening to the man with the gun. He continued to approach, glancing often up and down Newville Road for signs of danger, totally unaware that he was walking into a trap.

"I couldn't find the last one," the man said, when he was close enough to communicate without shouting. "It made it across the creek, and . . ."

He broke off in mid-sentence when he noticed Mercer lying there.

"What's goin' on?" he asked, a puzzled look on his face.

Mercer rolled to his feet and displayed his badge again.

"State game warden, you're under arrest," he said. "Lay the rifle down." The man hesitated and backed up a step, his puzzled look turning to one of fear.

"Lay it down," repeated Mercer, as Hiller approached from one side.

The suspect looked over at Hiller and back at Mercer, then carefully laid the rifle at his feet.

With three of the four suspects now in custody, and no indication that there were any others, the wardens separated the suspects and questioned them one at a time. Two of them refused to say much of anything, but the third, the youngest of the group, said a lot.

According to the younger one, he had been talked into going with the other three men to shoot deer to sell in the city. He claimed that he was just along for the ride, and that he had no idea where the deer were to be sold. He said that his companions had shot the deer from their car, using a spotlight, the plan being to knock down as many as they could, then go back later to field dress them.

Mercer was curious about where the men had parked their car and why they had spent part of the night in the barley field. The talkative suspect explained that they had parked their car near the cemetery. Mercer cringed at the realization that he and Hiller, in the dark, had parked the patrol car within a stone's throw of the poacher's vehicle. But the poachers had been down in the barley field working on their deer, and when their flashlights went dead, they had simply huddled in some deep grass to wait for dawn. Mercer asked the talkative one the name of the suspect who escaped, but at that point the man's memory suddenly went bad.

Since the wardens had five deer to transport back to town, and since the suspects were all locals, the wardens seized the gun and spotlight into evidence and issued citations to the three men—this instead of booking them into county jail. After being released by the wardens, it was a dejected-looking trio of deer poachers that trudged back to their car.

Now the work began. It was bad enough cramming five deer and two wardens into one patrol car, but when the wardens found three more deer in a field closer to Leo Flood's place, they really had problems. When they finally limped into Orland later that morning, there were parts of deer sticking out the windows and doors, and the patrol car was riding perilously low to the ground.

From Orland, it was on to Willows, for they had decided to drop the deer off at the Glenn County Jail.

"I hope those inmates like venison," Hiller said, "because that's all they're gonna be eatin' for the next month."

Mercer took a moment to add up their score for the past twelve hours. They had captured three out of four of the worst deer poachers they had encountered in a long time, and they had recovered a total of eight deer. "Not a bad night's work," he thought.

When their evidence was secured and the wardens were back in the patrol car, Hiller, a twinkle in his eye, turned to Mercer and said, "If we hurry, Saber, we can still make it back in time to help the captain paint his cabin."

"Yeah, sure," answered Mercer with a grin, ". . . or we could sprout wings and fly."

Strange Hiding Places

Mercer was totally puzzled as he stood staring at the gray sedan at the side of the road, its four doors standing wide open. He scratched his head in dismay as he considered the situation. A pheasant was hidden somewhere in that car—he was certain of it. But so far, the search had turned up nothing.

On the opposite side of the vehicle, Warden Garrie Heryford was having similar thoughts. He and Mercer had searched the car from one end to the other, looking under the seats, all through the trunk, and even in the engine compartment, but to no avail. The shotgun was there with a half box of shells, but no pheasant.

A young mother-to-be occupied the front passenger seat of the vehicle, while her husband stood by the left-front fender, fidgeting nervously with his hands, anxiously watching every move the wardens made.

"Can't we go now?" he asked. "We're not hiding anything."

The two wardens had been on patrol in the farm country south of Chico when they first spotted the sedan. A distant gunshot drew their attention to it, and Mercer located it with his massive pair of brass Bausch and Lomb binoculars. Although more than a mile away,

Mercer watched as a man emerged from the vehicle and ran out into a field and retrieved something. Mercer was certain—based on the location, the man's actions, and the season—that it was a pheasant.

It took several minutes to approach the sedan and make the stop. During part of that time, the sedan had been out of sight, which would have been time enough for the man to have hidden the pheasant anywhere in the vehicle—or even thrown it out, had he felt threatened. But Mercer was fairly certain that he and Heryford had surprised the man and wife, and from the looks of both of them—the woman in particular appeared to be terrified—they were still hiding something in the vehicle.

Mercer walked over to the driver's door and looked in again, scrutinizing the floor in front of the seat. He was about to begin another, more systematic search of the entire vehicle when he spotted something on the floor near the woman's feet. It was a feather. He walked quickly around to the front passenger door, reached in, and picked it up. It was a flank feather of a rooster pheasant.

"That's from last pheasant season!" the man exclaimed, starting around the car towards Mercer.

"Stay where you are," ordered Mercer, directing the man back to the front of the car.

Mercer then looked into the car again, directing his attention to the woman. She would not meet his eyes, looking instead straight ahead out the windshield, her hands clasped tightly across her swollen abdomen. Then it dawned on Mercer.

"Ma'am, would you please step out of the car," he said. It was a demand, not a question.

"Wait a minute," protested the husband. "She's been sick, I don't want her out . . ."

"Step out, please," Mercer repeated, ignoring the man.

The women looked up at Mercer, then swung her legs out and struggled awkwardly to her feet, still holding her hands across her stomach.

"Give us the pheasant," Mercer instructed, looking straight into her eyes.

"What pheasant? I don't have any pheasant," the woman cried.

Mercer then pointed to her stomach and said, "If you don't give it to us now, we'll take you to county jail and have a matron get it for us."

The woman looked over at her husband, who just shrugged his shoulders, then back at Mercer. Seeing that it was no use to put off the inevitable, she turned her back to the wardens, bent over, reached up under her dress and pulled out a freshly killed rooster pheasant.

*　　　　　*　　　　　*

Nearly as unusual was a case that occurred in Plumas County when Mercer was still the warden in Portola. After receiving information that a man had poached a deer and had the animal hanging at his home in Silver Valley, Mercer and Warden Oscar Schumaker went there with a search warrant.

The patrol car plowed through a foot of snow to get to the cabin at the upper end of the valley. The wardens were met at the door by their prime suspect, the owner of the place.

"We understand you have a deer here someplace," said Mercer, after he and Schumaker identified themselves. "We're gonna have to see it."

"Deer?" queried the suspect, in mock surprise. "Not me, you must be mistaken."

"Well, at any rate, we have a search warrant to search your house," Mercer explained. "So, if you don't mind, we'll go on in and take a look around."

The two wardens started up the steps to the front door.

"Wait a minute," the suspect said, holding one hand up in a stop gesture. "You can't go in there, my wife's sick."

"Put her in the bedroom," said Mercer. "We're comin' in."

"All right," said the suspect, "but it'll take me just a minute."

The wardens gave the suspect his minute, then walked on into the house and began their search. Checking all but the bedroom, they found nothing inside the house. Schumaker, however, found a smear of fresh blood on the back porch. A further search of the back porch and the woodshed failed to produce the deer, which the wardens were now sure was close by.

"It's obvious you've got a deer hidden around here somewhere," said Mercer. "You'd better give it to us now."

But the man denied knowledge of any deer, claiming that the blood on the back porch was from some fresh beef that had been given to them.

"We're gonna have to look in the bedroom," said Mercer. "Tell your wife to cover up."

"Hey, that's goin' too far," the suspect cried. "You're gonna upset her, and she's really sick."

"Tell her to cover up," Mercer repeated, heading for the bedroom door.

The woman of the house was in bed, on her back, the bedcovers drawn up tightly under her chin. She stared out at Mercer with frightened eyes. Mercer looked first in the closet, then under the bed. The deer was nowhere to be seen, but he did find a single drop of blood. He was getting close.

He stood back for a second, looking for somewhere that the deer could be hidden. Then it came to him. He looked again at the woman in the double bed, scrutinizing the lumps and bumps under the covers. There were too many lumps and bumps.

Seeing the look of realization on Mercer's face, the woman knew that it was all over. She quickly slipped out of bed—fully clothed—and stomped out of the room.

"I've had enough of this, Harold," she wailed. "I'm through lying for you."

Mercer walked over to the bed and threw the covers

back. There was the evidence—the woman had been sharing her bed with a spike buck.

*   *   *

On another occasion, in the mountains above Oroville, the evidence turned out to be much more difficult to retrieve. Mercer had enlisted the help of wardens Ed Johnston and Ros Tinnin to go with him on a deer investigation at a small Indian settlement near Bald Rock. Mercer had received word that one of the Indians, known locally as Bald Rock Charlie, had killed a deer the day before, and while the information was too sketchy for a search warrant, Mercer wanted to go there anyway to see if he could come up with something.

The three wardens arrived shortly before noon. The settlement—occupying a small clearing on a wooded ridge, beneath the huge, nearly bare formation of gray granite known as Bald Rock Dome—was hardly more than a cluster of wooden shacks. A motley collection of dogs came rushing out at the patrol car, giving the wardens a noisy reception as they pulled to a stop in front of what appeared to be the main building.

A half dozen children stood watching as the wardens stepped out of the patrol car, and several women looked up from their work and stared sullenly at the intruders. The wardens noticed there were no men in sight.

"Where's Charlie?" Mercer asked, directing the question at a middle-aged woman bent over a washboard in a galvanized tub.

"What do you want?" asked a male voice, as a squat, heavy-limbed Indian appeared in the doorway of the nearest shack.

He was of indeterminate age, with straight black hair that fell well below his shoulders. His weathered face, the color of polished walnut, bore an unfriendly expression, punctuated with coal black, hostile eyes. He reminded Mercer of a photograph he had once seen of an Apache warrior.

"We heard you killed a deer, Charlie," said Mercer.

"Well, you heard wrong," answered Charlie.

"If that's the case, you won't mind if we have a look around," said Mercer.

"Well, I do mind," said Charlie. "Do you have a search warrant?"

"No, but we can get one," said Mercer, who had noticed one of the dogs guarding what appeared to be the fresh front leg bones of a deer.

"Then you better go get one," said Charlie.

Since Charlie was uncooperative, the wardens had no choice but to go after a search warrant, a process that would take some time. Luckily, the deer bones Mercer had spotted would provide the extra 'probable cause' the wardens needed to get the warrant. It was agreed that Ros Tinnin would go after the warrant, while Mercer and Johnston waited at the settlement. Tinnin was soon on his way in the patrol car.

When Tinnin left for the warrant, Mercer remained with Charlie in front while Johnston positioned himself to watch the rear of the collection of shacks. This was necessary to prevent anyone from sneaking off with the deer meat the wardens were certain was somewhere inside.

Three hours later, Tinnin returned with the warrant, and the wardens proceeded with the search. In what was obviously a meat-hanging room screened in under a stairway, they found fresh blood and meat drippings, but no deer. They continued to search, going through all the shacks. Still no deer. They were greatly puzzled, for the evidence was indisputable.

They stood back, pondering the situation, then Mercer had a thought. While he and Johnston had been waiting for Tinnin to return with the warrant, he had noticed several of the women making trips down a well-trodden path, across a heavy plank bridging a small creek, to the outhouse in plain sight on the hillside. And now that he thought about it, there had been too many such trips.

Grabbing his flashlight, he hurried over to the outhouse, propped the door open, and had a look. Sure enough, peering down through the egg-shaped hole, he could see deer meat, easily forty pounds of it, amid the filth at the bottom of the pit. The women had cut the meat into pieces, hidden it under their clothing, and smuggled it out of the shacks.

Mercer walked back outside, informed the other wardens of his find, then walked down to the creek. Choosing a long, fairly straight willow branch, he hacked it off with his knife and carved one end to a needle point. A few inches above the point, he cut a small barb, and then, after hefting it once or twice in his right hand, he nodded his head in satisfaction and started back to the outhouse.

Tinnin and Johnston looked on, much amused, as Mercer—in much the same way as winter fishermen spear pike through the ice—jabbed at the pieces of deer meat mired below. An old woman, watching from nearby, broke into a toothless grin and cackled merrily as Mercer emerged from the outhouse, his face contorted into a grimace, a piece of filth-covered venison skewered on the end of his spear. He held it at arms length and walked quickly to the creek where he stirred it around vigorously in the water. After repeating the process and spearing a second piece of meat, he gingerly wrapped the foul-smelling evidence in some rags and put it in the trunk of the patrol car.

When he returned from the patrol car, he had his citation book with him, and Bald Rock Charlie received a citation for killing deer out of season. Charlie was indignant about the whole thing.

"My people have been killing deer around here for thousands of years," said Charlie.

"That's true," said Mercer. "But they didn't use .30-30 rifles."

Charlie signed his citation, received his copy, and the wardens went on their way.

A Mink for Marge

It was a winter morning in the marshland, and the sun was finally burning its way through the dense veil of tule fog that had shrouded the north valley for over a week. Mercer was working his way south through the farm country, patrolling the waterfowl areas he had worked each winter for the past eighteen years. Southbound on Seven Mile Lane, near Nelson West Road, he spotted a new sedan partially hidden off the road behind a stand of willows. It was an odd place for a duck hunter to park.

"That doesn't belong there," thought Mercer, eyeing the vehicle as he drove by. Although tempted to slow down for a better look, he maintained a steady speed so as to attract no more attention than any other passing motorist. He traveled another half mile before slowing his patrol car and turning around. He then slipped back into the area and concealed his car behind an old barn.

It was the tail end of duck season in 1956, and with the closing day at hand, Mercer felt as though a great weight was about to be lifted from his shoulders. True enough, there would still be poaching problems after the season closed, but at least the crowds of legitimate duck and goose hunters would be elsewhere. For Mercer and the other waterfowl wardens, it was a time to breathe a little easier.

Mercer stepped around to the front of the barn and peered up Seven Mile toward the hidden sedan. The remaining fog still obscured his vision, but he could hear a large flock of ducks feeding in the southeast corner of the large piece of land known as the Parrott Grant. He was certain that the flock of ducks had something to do with the presence of the hidden sedan.

Just then, as if to confirm his suspicion, a series of five rapid shots rang out, and the flock of ducks lifted skyward. As always, there was a second or two with only the roar of the multitudes of beating wings before the birds broke into their wild chorus of excited calls. And as always, Mercer was heartsick at the thought of the wasteful destruction that resulted when shotguns were fired into dense numbers of frightened waterfowl.

Mercer trained his binoculars in the direction of the shooting, but could see nothing but the departing ducks. Foliage along a canal that formed the southern boundary of the Parrott Grant made it impossible for him to see anything on the ground beyond it. Without further hesitation, he set out at a fast walk through the barley stubble.

Arriving at the canal, he located a break in the willows and was about to cross, when he spotted a man struggling in his direction under a load of ducks. Mercer dropped to the ground and crawled under some brush as the suspect approached. The man appeared highly nervous, glancing often toward Seven Mile Lane. Upon reaching the canal, the man eased himself down the bank and waded across, depositing the ducks on the opposite shore only a few feet from Mercer. Then, after a quick look around, the suspect hurried back the way he had come.

Mercer made no attempt to stop him, figuring the man would return shortly with more ducks. This proved to be the case, and as the suspect arrived with his second load, Mercer got a better look at him.

"That's Harold Hobbs," thought Mercer, recognizing the man. Hobbs was a well-known Chico businessman.

Mercer, from his hiding place in the tules, studied the man. There was something about Hobbs' appearance that made him look out of place in the marsh. Although he was dressed from head to toe in hunter's clothing, he looked like anything but a hunter. He appeared instead to be completely out of his element. His face was flushed with exertion, and yet there was a certain indoor pallor that persisted.

"He's definitely more at home behind his desk makin' money," thought Mercer.

By the time Hobbs headed back for his third load of ducks, the fog had lifted and Mercer could watch him trudge all the way back to where he had shot into the flock. With the whole scene now in view, Mercer could see the dry ditch that had allowed Hobbs to stay out of sight as he approached the ducks.

"He must have been right in the middle of 'em," thought Mercer, as he watched Hobbs picking up more ducks. "I wonder how many of 'em he just crippled?"

Even from more than a hundred yards away, Mercer could see dead ducks scattered all over the field. He had the choice of either waiting for Hobbs to gather all the birds and carry them across the canal to where he was waiting, or he could make contact now and help with the work. But since the latter option involved crossing the canal—which was certainly too deep for his hip boots—he chose to wait.

With some time to kill, he leaned back, making himself a little more comfortable in his tule nest. In the sky above him, many of the ducks were still milling around, looking for a new place to set down, and a flight of sandhill cranes was leisurely winging their way by, singing their ancient and stirring song. In the canal, a few feet from where he lay, a muskrat went sculling by, its eyes and whiskered nose barely above water. Closer yet, to Mercer's delight, a marsh wren hopped busily through a maze of bulrushes, announcing his presence with his raspy, twittering call. These were things that Mercer loved—his overtime pay for the countless, otherwise unpaid hours he devoted to the job he loved. And it was pay enough, for after more than twenty-eight years of intense warden work, he still looked forward to each new day.

Hobbs made a few more round trips, adding more ducks to the growing pile on Mercer's side of the canal. Then, finally, he returned with only a few ducks in one hand and an expensive shotgun in the other. After slogging his way across the canal for the last time and tossing the ducks into the pile, he placed the shotgun on some dry tules and sat down wearily for a rest. Mercer chose that moment to make his move.

"Good morning, Mr. Hobbs," he said, rising to his feet less than fifteen feet away.

Hobbs gave a violent start and whirled around. At the sight of the warden, his normally pale visage went *totally* devoid of color.

"Looks like you got a little greedy this morning," continued Mercer.

But Hobbs couldn't answer. He sat gasping for breath, feeling as though some giant hand had a grip on his heart.

"Take it easy, you're gonna be all right," said Mercer, suddenly concerned that he may have frightened the man into a coronary.

Slowly Hobbs recovered enough to talk. Looking at the pile of ducks, he said, "I don't know why I did it ... or what got into me. They were just so close..."

Mercer had seen it before—basically law-abiding men yielding to the temptation to ground-shoot into a flock of resting waterfowl. The experience of being within shotgun range of thousands of ducks apparently stirred some primeval hunter's instinct in some men to kill beyond reason. Mercer thought it was probably the same instinct that prompted ancient hunters to drive entire herds of bison over cliffs.

Mercer counted the ducks and wasn't at all surprised when the number totaled well over a hundred.

"I really feel bad," said Hobbs. "I didn't mean to kill this many."

"Well, let's get going," said Mercer, "We've got to get these birds over to my car."

When the ducks were packed away in Mercer's patrol car, he issued Hobbs a citation and seized his engraved Browning shotgun into evidence. Because of the serious nature of the violation, and because Hobbs was a well-known and respected Chico resident, Mercer cited him to appear in federal court. It was a logical decision, for Mercer had absolutely no doubts as to what would happen to the case in the local courts.

Three weeks later, Mercer encountered Hobbs in Chico. Expecting a cold reception, he was surprised when Hobbs greeted him with a smile and a handshake.

"I want you to know," said Hobbs, "that I don't blame you at all for catching me. You were just doin' your job, and I had it coming."

"I appreciate that," answered Mercer, who genuinely respected a person who could get caught and take his medicine like a man.

"My little duck hunt ended up costing me over a thousand dollars," continued Hobbs. Mercer winced at the figure, for he had expected the fine to be far less.

"Yes," continued Hobbs, "The judge only fined me five hundred dollars, but when Marge, my wife, found out about it, she figured that if I could spend that much on duck hunting, then she ought to be able to spend that much on herself. So, she went out and bought herself a new mink coat."

Bad Day for Berg

James Campbell looked with pride upon his master-piece of iron and steel. It was an awesome sight, its massive beams and girders spanning a rugged canyon that would soon be inundated by the rising waters of Lake Oroville. Known as the West Branch Bridge, it was being built to carry the new Highway 70, which was being rerouted due to the construction of Oroville Dam. James Campbell was supervising engineer of the project.

Campbell had arrived early that morning, well ahead of the construction crews, to attend to some things that were easier done when he was alone. He was peering through a transit when, suddenly, he was startled by a rifle shot up the canyon to the north.

"That was pretty close," he thought, as he hurried over to his truck for his binoculars. Walking out onto the half-finished bridge, he looked up the canyon a half mile to where the old Yankee Hill Road snaked its way down one canyon wall, crossed the West Branch River, and continued up the opposite side. Scanning the road with his binoculars, he spotted a car stopped at one of the switchbacks, and there were two men dragging something back into the brush. One of the men then returned to the car and lifted the hood to the engine compartment—as though he were having car trouble—and waited. Ten minutes later, the second man appeared, empty-handed, and they closed the hood and drove away.

Certain that he had just witnessed the illegal killing of a deer, Campbell hurried back to his truck and drove down to the schoolhouse at Pentz to use the telephone.

It was around 7 A.M. when Mercer got the call. He knew at once that Campbell's report was on the level, and upon hearing that the poachers had stashed the deer, he headed out immediately. Less than a half hour later, he was standing on the West Branch Bridge and Campbell was pointing out the spot where the violation had occurred. Fifteen minutes after that, he was standing in a small clearing along Yankee Hill Road, staring down at a patch of blood-soaked earth.

"This is where it fell," he thought, examining the scars scratched in the ground by flailing hooves. "Must have been a head or a neck shot."

Following bloody drag marks into the brush, he found the deer under a large manzanita bush. It was a small spike buck, field dressed, its body cavity propped open with a stick. There was no doubt the poachers planned to return for it. Leaving the deer where it lay, Mercer hurried back to his patrol car and drove out of the canyon.

Unfortunately, the deer was stashed in a spot that was hard to watch, for Mercer could only cover the road leading in from one side of the canyon. He would need another warden to cover the other side. Reaching for his radio microphone, he tried without success to call the adjoining wardens, then finally succeeded in reaching Warden Gill Berg of Gridley. Berg had been up all night the night before, but readily agreed to help and arrived on the scene in less than an hour.

Now, Mercer and Gill Berg had known each other for a long time and had worked together from time to time over the years, and it was well known that their philosophies concerning game-warden work were often at odds. In fact, it is generally believed that it was Berg who first dubbed Mercer 'Sabertooth,' no doubt as a result of some biting criticism he received from the sharp-tongued warden. But Berg was a highly entertaining person, good-natured and well liked by everybody. He was an excellent storyteller with a well-tuned sense of humor, and whenever wardens got together, and Berg was around, he usually kept the others in stitches. There was no doubt about it, Berg was good company.

But Mercer wasn't looking for good company that day. He just wanted someone to watch one side of the canyon while he watched the other. When Berg arrived, Mercer sent him across to a spot from which he could watch part of Yankee Hill Road and the other approaches to the illegal deer that were obscured from Mercer's view. When Berg was in position, they settled down to wait.

The hours passed slowly, and, since it turned out to be a warm day, Mercer became concerned that the deer might spoil. The more he thought about it, the more it bothered him, so around noon he drove down to do something about it. From the trunk of his patrol car he removed a new, burlap wool-sack, more than six feet long. It made a perfect game bag and he had been delighted when he had acquired it, only a few weeks earlier. Hurrying to the deer, he quickly pulled the wool-sack over it, tied it shut, and pushed the bundle farther back under the manzanita to protect it from the sun. A few minutes later, he was back at his lookout spot on the ridge.

The afternoon dragged by and Mercer was puzzled that the poachers hadn't returned. "They must know we're here," he thought, but decided to give the stakeout another hour or two. At dusk, he had to admit that the poachers weren't coming back. It had been just too long. He gave a sigh of frustration as he headed the patrol car back down into the canyon to pick up the deer. On the way down, he called Berg on the radio, advised him of the situation, and thanked him for his help. Berg immediately started back for Gridley.

Mercer parked off the roadway and walked back through the brush to retrieve the deer. But when he reached the manzanita bush, he stopped cold. The blood was there, the pile of entrails was there ... but the deer was gone. He looked around frantically, as though doubting his senses, but the deer simply was not there.

He was furious as he stomped back to the patrol car. "I can't believe it," he fumed. "They got it right out from under our damned noses." Then he thought about his wool-sack and his rage doubled. Arriving back at his patrol car, he grabbed his microphone.

"Berg, where the hell have you been?" he raged, with little regard for radio etiquette. "They got the deer and they got my wool-sack."

"I didn't see 'em come by me," answered Berg lamely.

"Well they *had* to come by you ... you must have been asleep," shouted Mercer.

While this exchange was anything but pleasant for Berg, there were others who found it thoroughly entertaining—other wardens who happened to be out with their radios on. Many had heard it and thought it was hilarious, and it became a main topic of conversation for weeks.

As Mercer expected, it wasn't long before he learned through the grapevine who had been responsible for killing the deer. The word was that it had been a couple of young poachers from Lake Concow. The way they were telling the story, they had returned on foot to carry the deer to another nearby road where it would be less risky to load it into a car, but on their way to the deer, they had blundered onto a game warden, asleep in his car. Shaken at first, they were ready to forget about the whole thing, but then it dawned on them what a great joke it would be to go ahead and sneak by the sleeping warden and pick up the deer. And apparently that's exactly what they did.

While Berg adamantly denied that he was ever asleep during the stakeout, there seemed to be no better explanation for what happened, and the other wardens teased him unmercifully about it. Each of them knew very well the treatment they would have received from Berg had it been them that dozed off—an easy thing to do on a long stakeout on a warm afternoon after being up all night—so they got all the mileage they could out of the incident. In fact, at a squad meeting not long thereafter, a group of grinning wardens presented Berg with a book—a large volume entitled:

All I Have Learned About Stakeouts
By Gill Berg

Opening the book, Berg found to his dismay that it contained absolutely nothing . . . every page was totally blank.

Callin' It
Quits

It was a sad day for Patrol Captain David Nelson of the California Department of Fish and Game. He had come to Chico, that thirty-first day of August, 1962, to complete a chore that was weighing heavily on him. Warden Gene Mercer was retiring, and there were final details to attend to.

What made it so hard for Nelson was the fact that Mercer was no ordinary warden. For more than thirty years, he had been so dedicated, so hardworking, and so effective that he was believed by many—Nelson included—to be one of a kind. And not only had he become somewhat of a legend in the north part of the state, but he had become a valued friend to Dave Nelson.

Now, Nelson had been around long enough to have seen a good many wardens retire. Most had been more than ready when the time came, and while it was often an emotional experience for them, there were seldom any strong regrets. But such was not the case this day with Mercer.

Nelson sat at the kitchen table of Mercer's modest home in a quiet part of town. Across from him sat Old Sabertooth himself, probably the finest game warden he had ever known. The aging officer, still lean and hard, with those same penetrating brown eyes, sat staring down at the badge he held in his hand, the symbol of the profession that had dominated his life for so many years. On the table between the two men was a pair of battered binoculars, a pair of handcuffs, the keys to a patrol car, and a few other articles of state equipment that Nelson had come to collect.

Nelson regarded his old friend with concern.

"Are you sure you're doing the right thing, Pappy?" he asked, using the affectionate nickname that only he and a few others were privileged to use.

"Yes, Dave, my mind's made up," Mercer replied, and Nelson knew that the matter was settled.

What most bothered Nelson was the fact that Mercer wasn't ready to retire. He still had more energy and enthusiasm for the job than most wardens half his age. But circumstances were forcing him into it—or at least that's how Mercer saw it. Nelson knew that there would be no changing his mind, and was gravely concerned that the tough old guy wouldn't last long without his work.

Mercer had been disgruntled for several months, upset with changes in the department. He was particularly upset over the new restrictions on work hours. Not only were they going to limit him to eight hours a day, but they were now going to make him take two days off every week. He was outraged. He found the new policy stifling and unacceptable.

On top of this, he had health problems. Two years earlier, he had suffered a stroke, and the doctors had told him then that if he wanted to live, he would have to quit his job immediately. Even then, if he took it easy, they gave him a maximum of eight or nine more years. He had ignored them, but since that time, he had been plagued by the nagging feeling that he should be spending more of his remaining time with his wife and family, instead of out chasing violators.

Then, too, in recent months, he had begun feeling that he was no longer doing justice to the job, an opinion definitely not shared by his supervisors. Despite his working long hours, and his continuing to work on his days off on the sly, his caseload was gradually falling—he wasn't catching as many violators. This greatly worried him. As he explained it, "Things just aren't clicking anymore."

Dave Nelson, however, knew better. It was the poachers who were slowing down, not Mercer.

Nelson smiled to himself as he remembered a heated discussion during a Warden's Association meeting in San Francisco, some ten years earlier. He couldn't recall the issue, but he remembered well Mercer's memorable statement, "I may not be the *best* damned warden in the state . . . but I'm *one* of the best!"

It was a true statement, and no one there could argue the point.

"But the fact is," thought Nelson, "it's still true."

Nelson knew, with absolute certainty, that Gene Mercer—even at age sixty-two, on the last day of a career that had spanned more than thirty-four years, and despite a body that was beginning to fail him—was still one of the finest Fish and Game wardens in the state. Things would never be the same without him.

Warden Gene 'Sabertooth' Mercer gazed fondly at the six-pointed star of sterling silver, with its blue enamel lettering encircling the gold seal of California, the state he loved and had served so well. He tossed it once in his palm, then carefully placed it on the table and pushed it over to Nelson . . . and with the badge went a piece of his heart.

Author's Postscript

At the time of this writing, a quarter century after his retirement, Gene Mercer is living with his daughter in Sacramento. But it took a long time for him to truly retire. His *official* retirement didn't even last a day. He turned in his badge on the day before the opening of dove season, 1962, and Captain Dave Nelson was surprised to receive a phone call from him that same evening.

"I know where there'll be a lot of doves tomorrow," said Mercer. "It'll be a good bet for overlimits . . . What time are you gonna pick me up?"

The following morning, his first day of 'retirement,' he was out before daybreak with Captain Nelson, doing what he had done every September first for over thirty years—working dove hunters.

Years later, in 1976, when I arrived in Butte County, Mercer was not only patrolling with the local wardens every chance he got, but he had also become the secretary to the Butte County Fish and Game Commission. He was again directly involved in looking after wildlife. He remained the highly active, highly outspoken secretary to the commission until the spring of 1982 when, after fourteen years, he finally called it quits.

But he continued to ride with the wardens. In the fall of 1987, twenty-four years to the day after his retirement, I shared one last dove-opener sunrise with him in a harvested field along the Sacramento River. Although I didn't know it at the time, it would be his last patrol. At age eighty-five, the years were finally catching up with him. We stood together in the gathering light as the first flocks of doves rocketed by and the distant popping of shotgun fire began. I couldn't help but steal a glance his way. He was in his element, tasting again the things he loved best. He reminded me of an embattled old grizzly sniffing the breeze, one of the last of his breed, a relic from days gone forever. But there was still life in Old Sabertooth. He stared up at the sky with rapt attention, his eyes alive with excitement, burning with the old fire of years past.

It was a moving experience for me, that September morning along the river—an experience I won't soon forget.

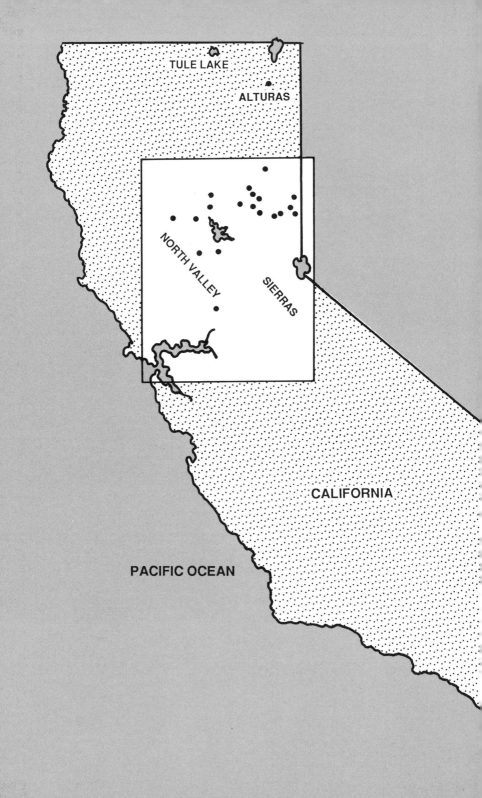